THE CHILI COOKBOOK

THE
CHILI
COOKBOOK

A HISTORY OF THE ONE-POT CLASSIC, WITH COOK-OFF WORTHY RECIPES FROM THREE-BEAN TO FOUR-ALARM AND CON CARNE TO VEGETARIAN

ROBB WALSH

PHOTOGRAPHY BY EVA KOLENKO

TEN SPEED PRESS
Berkeley

FOR THE WALSH BROTHERS

Scott, David, Gordon, Rick, and Mike
" . . . he who eats the fastest gets the most!"

CONTENTS

Robert Redford's Lamb Chili with Black Beans (page 157)

INTRODUCTION

If chili is enjoying a revival lately, it's not the second coming—more like the third or fourth, depending on when you start counting. The history of chili con carne is deep, dark, and very complicated.

Mexicans, Texans, New Mexicans, and Midwesterners have been arguing about chili for well over a century. They are still debating what it is, how to spell it, and who invented it. Other subjects of contention include: one "L" or two in the middle, "I" or "E" on the end; tomato versus no tomato, beans versus no beans, ground meat versus hand chopped, and disputes about spices so arcane, they defy rational explanation.

As a partner in a Tex-Mex restaurant where we serve gallons and gallons of Texas chili every day, I have to confess that I am not an objective observer. But as a student of food history and an enthusiastic consumer, I put my preconceptions aside long enough to research this book. And I was richly rewarded with good chili from unexpected places and amazing (sometimes true) tales.

This book delves into the five hundred years of chili history beginning with the Aztec chile stews the conquistadors sampled in the markets of Montezuma in the 1500s and includes chili recipes inspired by the Spanish mission era of the 1700s, when the first chile peppers were cultivated in

North America and the cattle-herding traditions of the Texas cowboys were born.

Several chapters focus on Texas chili, including the San Antonio version of the 1800s, the heyday of the Chili Queens and the Chicago World's Fair of 1894 where Tex-Mex chili created a sensation. The spread of chili across the Midwest in the 1900s takes us for a trip down that highway of memory called Route 66. There are side trips to Ohio, Michigan, and Washington, DC. And finally, we return to the twenty-first century home kitchen, where chili has taken on a new identity as the most modern of American dishes.

If you love chili, you will probably find some of the recipes in this book comforting and some of them vexing, especially if you're a purist with firmly held ideas about beans or spaghetti or whatever. Suspend your disbelief for a just a bit and trust your taste buds.

The modern recipes in the book include lamb chilis, pork chilis, chicken chilis, shrimp chili, and yes, even a whole chapter on meatless chilis (because vegetarians have to eat, too). Recipes for Hungarian goulash, Pakistani keema, and Greek spaghetti sauce are also included as part of my argument that each has played a part in chili's colorful history.

Some of the cooking instructions are ridiculously simple, and some are more ambitious. Cooking methods have evolved from cast-iron pots on the campfire to the modern stovetop, and now include convenient slow-cooker variations that you can start in the morning and eat when you get home from work.

Read a few of the stories and try a few of the recipes collected here, and you may come to the same conclusion I did—that chili is both a quintessential American dish and a part of an ancient chile pepper culture that has become deeply ingrained in the whole world's cooking.

CHILI KITCHEN NOTES

Before we get started, let's make sure we're all on the same page when it comes to equipment and ingredients.

Equipment Most recipes in this book call for a Dutch oven, meaning a heavy-duty pot with a 5- to 7-quart capacity and a lid. You can substitute a soup pot, stew pot, or any other vessel that comfortably holds the amount of chili you require, but to avoid burning, I recommend cast-iron, enamelware, or any heavy-duty pot made with multiple layers of metal, such as All-Clad. Most chilis do extremely well in the slow-cooker (see box on page 3).

Ratio The basic ratio of ingredients that go into a well-seasoned chili was established by spice manufacturer and chili pioneer William Gebhardt (see page 46). His formula calls for 2 pounds of meat to 1 ounce (4 tablespoons) of chili powder to 4 cups of liquid. Standard additions include garlic, onions, and canned tomatoes.

Meats Beef was central to the old-fashioned chilis of the nineteenth century; however, even in those days venison and bison were common alternatives. Turkey chile stew goes back to the pre-Columbian era. Pork and lamb are excellent modern choices. In other words, use what you have or what inspires you.

Meat Prep In the earliest days of chili, meats were chopped or minced by hand, but ground meats have become more typical and are certainly convenient. "Chili grind" is a term used by Texas butchers to describe meats that have been coarsely ground using a ½-inch plate. It is ideal if you are looking for a more old-school texture but don't want to go to the trouble of hand-chopping your meat.

Masa Harina Masa harina is a powder that's used to make the dough for corn tortillas (page 25). It's also a favorite thickener in Texas-style chili con carne. The most common brand of masa harina in Mexico and the United States is Maseca; it's available in any grocery store that sells Mexican ingredients.

Serving Size For the recipes in this book, one serving of chili is a generous ½ cup. Figure on using a ¼ cup if you want an appetizer-size serving.

Leftovers and Storage Store leftover chili in a covered container in the refrigerator; it will keep for up to 4 days. In fact, chili is reputed to get better after sitting in the fridge for awhile. Chili freezes very well and can be kept for up to 3 months in the freezer. When preparing a large batch recipe, such as Homemade Coney Sauce (page 132), consider freezing the chili in several containers so you can thaw only the amount required.

CHILI IN THE SLOW-COOKER

This icon has been added to recipes that do well in a slow-cooker.

A long simmer time is ideal for many chilis and a 6-quart capacity slow-cooker will hold even the largest recipes in this book. If you want to cook chili all day while you are at work, just set the cooker on low—the chili meat will be fine.

If the recipe has beans, though, make sure to add the beans later. Canned beans will turn to mush if they cook too long. If you are cooking a chili that contains beans in an unattended slow-cooker, you will want to wait to add them 20 to 30 minutes before serving.

Some of the chilis in this book aren't right for a slow-cooker, so look for the icon.

CHILE IDENTIFICATION GUIDE

On the following pages, you'll find photos of the chiles used in this book. In the list below, they are in order from mildest to hottest.

DRIED CHILES

Ancho The dried form of the poblano chile, the ancho is also confusingly called a "pasilla" on both coasts. It is the fleshiest of the dried chiles, and its pulp combines a little bitterness with a sweetness reminiscent of raisins. This is the dried chile pepper that Gebhardt ground for his Eagle Brand Chili Powder, and it is still the chile pepper most often used in dark brown commercial chili powders such as McCormick Dark Chili Powder. Whether it is used as a pod or in its ground form, this is the chile that gives Texas chili its characteristic taste.

New Mexican Long Red Chile This tart, medium-hot pepper is sometimes used whole, but it is more often sold coarsely ground. The same chile is also called guajillo in Mexican markets. This is the chile pepper used in New Mexican red chile powder and in light chili powders. Beware—some guajillos from South America look like the New Mexican long red chile, but have no heat.

Pasilla Long and skinny with a slightly wrinkled, black skin, the pasilla has a strong, slightly bitter but satisfying flavor and can range from medium-hot to hot. The name is the diminutive of the Spanish word, *pasa*, meaning "raisin," a reference to the appearance of the skin.

Chipotle This is the smoke-dried jalapeño. Chipotles have an incredibly rich, smoky flavor and are usually very hot. The original Nahuatl spelling, *chilpotle*, is also sometimes seen. I prefer to use dry chipotles, but the widely available canned chipotles are acceptable in most recipes. Obviously, you can't make chile powder from canned chipotles, but you can use them for purees. Canned chipotles are already soaked in some kind of sauce, usually a vinegary adobo sauce. Just stem and seed them and puree them with some of the sauce from the can.

Japones Spanish for "Japanese," japones are also known as hontaka, santaka, or Chinese chiles, though they are actually native to Mexico. This easy-to-find dried chile is common in Asian, Latino, and other grocery stores. The brownish-red pointed pod averages 2 inches in length and imparts a very high heat. It's used in great quantities in Sichuan dishes. Cook-off competitor Wick Fowler floated one on top of each bowl of chili to impress cook-off judges and intimidate the uninitiated.

FRESH CHILES

New Mexican Long Green Chile This pepper was hybridized in the early 1900s to provide New Mexicans with a mild version of their native chile that could be eaten as a vegetable. It has a pleasant flavor and ranges from slightly warm to medium-hot. These chiles are generally roasted and peeled before they are used.

Modern cultivars of the New Mexican long green chile are grown from certified seed sources which are graded according to heat. "Hatch" chiles from the town of Hatch, New Mexico, are the most famous of the long green chiles, but an early cultivar of hybridized mild long green chile was transplanted to Southern California in the early 1900s where it became known as the Anaheim chile. The Anaheim name is common in much of the country. While the extremely mild Anaheim chile is less flavorful than the various Hatch cultivars, it is a suitable substitute.

Poblano Fatter and wider than the New Mexican long green chile, and sometimes called ancho or pasilla on both coasts, the poblano is a darker green color and has a richer flavor. It is one of the most commonly used chiles in Central Mexican cooking, both in its fresh and dried forms (see "Ancho" above). Poblanos are named after the Mexican city of Puebla. Generally, they are slightly hot and are usually roasted and peeled before use.

Jalapeño Hot, green, and bullet-shaped, the jalapeño is the classic American hot pepper and one of the world's best-known chiles. The Spanish named this chile after Jalapa (or Xalapa), a town in the state of Veracruz where it is grown. But the name is unpopular in the rest of Mexico due to the fact that the pepper is also grown in other places. In Mexico City, it is known as a *cuaresmeño* or *chile gordo*. The fresh jalapeño has a strong vegetal flavor to go with the heat.

Serrano The Spanish found this pepper in the mountains of Puebla and Hidalgo, so they named it serrano for the "*Sierras*" where it grew. Similar to the jalapeño, the serrano is hotter and smaller. Most Mexicans claim that serranos have a fuller, more herbaceous flavor.

Chile Pequín Also known as *piquín*, *chilipiquin*, or *chiltepin*, this tiny chile grows wild throughout southern Texas and northern Mexico. In northern Mexico, the chile is collected in the wild and sold in markets, where it fetches more than almost any other kind of chile. Chile pequíns are sometimes dried and preserved for year-round use. Because they are not grown commercially, they are seldom found in restaurant cooking or in grocery stores. They are available in Mexican markets in the early fall, however.

JALAPEÑO

POBLANO

NEW MEXICAN LONG
GREEN CHILE (ANAHEIM)

JAPONES

NEW MEXICAN
LONG RED CHILE
(GUAJILLO)

SERRANO

PASILLA

ANCHO

CHIPOTLE

RANKING CHILI POWDERS AND CHILI MIXES

There are a lot of chili powders, chili mixes, and other such preparations on the market. To sort them out, a few friends and I conducted a tasting of chili powders and chili mixes. Texas has some excellent liquid chili mixes that come in the same size bottles used for spaghetti sauces—but we skipped those because they aren't widely available.

For our tasting purposes, we sprinkled a generous amount of the spice over a small mound of mashed potatoes, mixed it in, and ate some.

CHILI POWDERS

Chili powders are proprietary blends of ground chiles and spices. Most chili powder manufacturers refuse to disclose what kind of chiles are in their bottles. The best chili powders are made with traditional and expensive ancho chiles or other high-quality chiles. Inferior blends use cheap paprika spiked with cayenne. It's hard to tell them apart by appearance, but there is a huge difference in flavor. Here are the brands we liked the best, in order of preference.

OUR TOP FIVE CHILI POWDERS

1 Gebhardt (classic ancho flavors and a little sweetness)

2 Bolner's Fiesta Fancy Light Chili Powder (bright red chile flavors)

3 Adam's (if you like it hot)

4 McCormick Dark Chili Powder (premium version of the national standard)

5 McCormick Chili Powder (the standard American chili powder)

OUR TOP FIVE CHILI MIXES

These seasoning mixes often contain granulated garlic and sometimes a thickener such as wheat flour or masa harina. Carroll Shelby's and Wick Fowler's companies market "Chili Kits." These contain multiple spice packets so the cook can customize the heat level, cumin level, and add thickeners or not. Here are our favorites.

1 Williams Original Chili Seasoning (pure, clean chile flavor)

2 Wick Fowler's 2-Alarm Chili Kit (customize it however you like)

3 Caroll Shelby's Original Texas Brand Chili Kit (another custom package)

4 Bolner's Fiesta Quick Chili Mix (salty with lots of garlic)

5 Pioneer Brand Chili Mix (strong cumin flavor)

MIXING YOUR OWN CHILI POWDER

Individual "chile powders" (such as ancho chile powder, chipotle chile powder, pasilla chile powder, and New Mexican red chile powder) are also available from spice companies. Using these pure ground chiles allows you to mix up a top-quality chili seasoning blend customized to the chili you are making.

For instructions on toasting and grinding spices to make a homemade chili powder, see the recipe on page 11.

HOMEMADE CHILI POWDER

Toasting chiles and cumin seeds in your own kitchen and grinding them in a spice grinder makes the best chili powder of all. This recipe calls for anchos, but you can use any combination of dried chiles.

MAKES ¼ CUP

5 whole dried ancho chiles (about 2 ounces)

1 teaspoon cumin seeds

1 teaspoon dried Mexican oregano, or to taste

½ teaspoon garlic powder

Remove the stems and seeds from the anchos and spread the peppers out flat. Reserve the seeds. Place the chiles flat on a *comal* or cast-iron skillet over medium heat. Being careful not to burn them, lightly toast until they are brittle, then remove and cool. Toast the cumin in the hot *comal*, stirring and shaking until fragrant. Toast some of the chile seeds, if desired. (The seeds will make the chili powder hotter.)

Cut the chiles into small strips with scissors. In a clean coffee grinder, grind the strips in several batches until powdered. Grind the cumin and chile seeds in the coffee grinder. Combine the powdered chile, ground seeds, Mexican oregano, and garlic powder in a mixing bowl. Grind the coarse powder in batches in the coffee grinder until fine, about 2 minutes. Store in an airtight container until ready to use.

PART 1

CHILI'S
FAMILY TREE

CHAPTER 1

LOBSTER CHILI IN OLD MEXICO

Lobster chili sounds like something from the menu of an upscale Southwestern cuisine restaurant. But the Franciscan friar Bernardino de Sahagún wrote about the dish and other details of Mesoamerican life in the *Florentine Codex*, published in 1529.

What did Aztec cooking taste like? I wondered as I strolled around Alameda Central, the vast and verdant park in the middle of Mexico City. The park was created in 1592 on the site of a market in the Aztec capital of Tenochtitlán. Maybe I was standing on the very spot where Spanish observers first sampled the Aztecs' lobster-chile stew.

In the Aztec market, Sahagún reported finding "hot green chiles, smoked chiles, water chiles, tree chiles, beetle chiles, and sharp-pointed red chiles." He also found strings of red chiles, cooked chiles, and "fish chiles" (an early form of *ceviche*). "They would eat another kind of stew, with frogs and green chile," Sahagún recorded, "and a stew of those fish called *axolotl* [Mexican salamander] with yellow chile."

"They also used to eat a lobster stew which is very delicious," he noted. The Spaniard was among the first Europeans to sample Mesoamerican wild turkey, which he recommended highly.

Chile was more than a favorite flavoring for Mesoamericans. Along with the vitamins and minerals contained in chile peppers, the peppers also acted as a preservative. In a paper titled "Darwinian Gastronomy: Why We Use Spices," two scientists postulate that early humans borrowed the chemical defenses of plants to combat microorganisms that spoiled the food. In this theory, humankind developed a taste for chiles and other beneficial spices as an evolutionary survival mechanism, because chiles kept the food from spoiling by inhibiting bacterial growth.

CHILE TAX

The importance of chiles in the Aztec culture was reflected in their system of taxation. Peasants were forced to a pay a portion of their crop in tribute to the emperor. Because they were so valuable, chiles were among the most common form of payment. The "chile tax" was paid in fresh or dried pods, seeds, dried chiles in two-hundred-pound bundles, in willow baskets, and in Spanish bushels. Records of Aztec tributes, such as those found in the *Mendocino Codex*, report that the Aztec town that became San Luis Potosi sent 1600 loads of dried chiles to the Aztec capital every year. San Luis Potosi is still a major source of dried anchos—a tradition that goes back at least five centuries.

Simmering meat in chile sauce was a well-developed part of Mesoamerican cookery long before the Spanish arrived. But the Spanish changed the kind of meat that went in the pot. After the Spanish brought European livestock to the Americas in the sixteenth century, pork, beef, and chicken became the most common ingredients in Mexican chile sauces.

The first mention in print of "chile con carne"—the stuff that most of us think of when we hear the word "chili"—is in an 1857 book about the Mexican-American War, titled *Chile con Carne; or the camp and the field*, written by S. Compton Smith, MD, acting surgeon with General Taylor's Division in Mexico. In the book, the Army doctor described an encampment under a grove of live oaks near Monterrey, where the locals "would assemble, and display their stock in trade, consisting usually of some carne seca and carne fresca, leche de cabro, chile con carne . . . " The doctor defined chile con carne as "a popular Mexican dish—literally red peppers and meat."

Based on this primary source, American food historians argue that chili is a Mexican dish. That might be convincing, if it weren't for an even earlier description of the dish from J. C. Clopper, a Texan visiting San Antonio in 1827, where he observed that poor *Tejanos* who could only afford small quantities of the cheapest beef "cut it into a hash with nearly as many peppers as there were pieces of meat."

As a matter of pride, modern-day Texans argue that chili isn't Mexican. And while there is ample evidence that the best-known version of the dish was actually invented in Texas, there is also plenty of evidence that Texans of the time thought of chili con carne as Mexican.

It's a paradox that we should be used to by now—the term "Tex-Mex" wasn't applied to food until the 1970s. Up until that time chili con carne, yellow cheese enchiladas, and the rest of the genre was known simply as "Mexican food."

"Chili con carne sounds authentically Spanish, which it could hardly be, for the Spaniards had never seen a chili [pepper] before they reached America; it was an element of Indian, not of Spanish, cooking. The Spanish name could have been explained by a Mexican origin, but the only persons who deny that provenance more vehemently than the Texans, who claim credit for it, are the Mexicans, who deny paternity with something like indignation."

—Waverly Root and Richard De Rochemont, *Eating in America: A History*

New Mexicans make the case that they invented the dish (although they spell it "chile"). And they have a point—in the 1600s, New Mexico was the first place in the present-day United States where chile peppers were cultivated. Chile peppers were being grown all over New Mexico by the time cattle ranching was getting started in Texas. Spanish herds imported in the 1720s became a big business in South Texas by the 1770s.

So which came first, the chile or the beef? Pinpointing the origin of chili con carne depends on how narrowly or broadly you define it. Mesoamericans were eating turkey, venison, and lobster (and a lot of other stuff) stewed in chile sauce before the arrival of Columbus. The red and green chile stews of New Mexico have also been around longer than Tex-Mex chili.

But there is no disputing that San Antonio chili con carne made with beef, dried chiles, and a large dose of cumin captured the imaginations and taste buds of much of the United States in the late 1800s and early 1900s. And it was the popularity of this dish that causes Texans to argue that this is the one true chili, and that it is not Mexican, but part of Tex-Mex, an American regional cuisine unique to Texas.

Where you stand on the issue hardly matters anymore; in the twenty-first century, the debate has become dated and irrelevant. The chili con carne craze that swept the nation a hundred years ago has come and gone. So has the revival sparked by the chili cook-offs of the 1970s. Spicy, beanless, old-fashioned Tex-Mex chili has receded to the borders of the Lone Star State.

And yet chili, as it is now more broadly defined, has never been more in fashion. A chili renaissance is under way. The dish is the new darling of the Americana cooking trend, a style that transforms traditional regional specialties into exciting modern dishes. In the process, the definition of chili has come unglued. In popular food culture, white chicken chili, green chile with pork, and black bean chili are now on an equal footing with the traditional Tex-Mex versions.

Which brings us full circle, back to the Aztec market where Sahagún sampled Mesoamerican chile stews in the 1500s. Texas purists like chili guru Joe Cooper, author of the 1952 seminal classic, *With or Without Beans*, would tell you that the lobster and chile stew of the sixteenth-century Aztecs had nothing to do with chili and can't be considered a part of the genre.

But food lovers of the twenty-first century ask: "Why not?"

ROASTED GREEN CHILES

Poblanos, Anaheims, and the long green chile of New Mexico have tough skins, so these chiles are usually roasted and the charred skins removed. Really, you can use this recipe to make as many roasted chiles as you want—whatever you don't use right away can be frozen easily for longer storage.

You can buy canned roasted and peeled green chiles in grocery stores year round, but they are so expensive that it's difficult to justify using them in large quantities.

MAKES 1 DOZEN

12 fresh New Mexican long green chiles, Anaheim chiles, or green poblano chiles

Rinse the fresh peppers and allow to dry. Set the oven to broil. Line a broiling pan or baking sheet with aluminum foil, place the chiles on top, and place the pan under the broiler. (The closer the pan is to the flame, the quicker the chiles will roast.) When the skin is well blistered and charred, after about 5 minutes, rotate the chiles to expose more green skin to the flame. Don't overdo it—if they turn completely black, there won't be any flesh left to cook with.

When the peppers are blistered all over, wrap them in wet paper towels, place them inside a plastic bag, and set it aside to steam gently for 10 to 15 minutes or until the skins are very loose.

When you remove the towels, most of the skin should come off easily. Scrape off the rest of the skin with a butter knife. Cut off the stem and remove the seeds with the side of a butter knife. (Don't rinse with water or you will lose a lot of flavor.)

Keep the roasted chiles in the refrigerator for up to 1 week, or freeze chiles for several months in packages containing four or five chiles each—enough for an average recipe.

LOBSTER CHILI

Here's a recipe I came up with while fantasizing about the Aztec lobster chili that Sahagún sampled in the 1520s. Granted, the Aztecs weren't eating Maine lobsters and their maize didn't look much like our corn on the cob, but you get the picture. Don't be too surprised if this ancient/modern chili is the tastiest you have ever eaten.

SERVES 4

4 (1¼-pound) lobsters

4 ears corn, shucked

12 cups water,
plus more as needed

12 roasted green chiles
(New Mexican long green
or poblano) (page 19)

1 serrano chile,
chopped (optional)

4 tatume squash or zucchini,
cut into ½-inch dice

1 white onion, chopped

1 teaspoon dried
Mexican oregano

2 tablespoons masa
harina dissolved in ¼ cup
hot water, to thicken,
plus more as needed

Salt

12 corn tortillas, homemade
(page 25) or store-bought

Pepper sauce, such as
Tabasco or Cholula

To cook the lobsters and corn, bring 12 cups of water to a boil over high heat in a soup pot large enough to fit the lobsters and corn (or use two pots). Put the lobsters and corn in the boiling water. Boil the lobsters until bright red, 10 to 12 minutes. Remove the lobsters and set aside to cool. Continue cooking the corn until tender, about 5 minutes more. Remove the corn and set aside to cool. Reserve the liquid.

When the lobsters are cool enough to handle, break off the claws, crack the claw shell and each joint with a nutcracker, and set aside. Remove the meat from the tail and chop into bite-size pieces and set aside. Remove the shell from the body and discard, making sure to reserve any greenish tomalley or red roe.

To make the stock, chop the body sections (where the legs connect to the body) in four parts (setting aside any easily removed lobster meat) and put the body pieces in the pot with the reserved liquid, along with any tomalley or roe. Bring to a boil, reduce to a simmer, and cook for 45 minutes, mashing with a potato masher frequently to extract as much lobster essence as possible. Add water as needed to maintain the level. Strain the liquid, you should have at least 10 cups.

To make the chili, combine 10 cups lobster stock, roasted green chiles, serrano, squash, onion, and oregano. Bring the stock to a boil, reduce to a simmer, and cook for 45 minutes, mashing with the

CONTINUED

potato masher until the squash and chiles begin to dissolve and the liquid reduces by a quarter. Do not puree. Add the masa harina mixture and stir to thicken. Add more masa dissolved in hot water, if needed, until the chili reaches the desired consistency. Salt to taste.

To serve, break each ear of corn into three pieces and add to the pot along with the lobster meat and claws to reheat for a minute or two. Then divide the chili among four large soup bowls, making sure the lobster meat is distributed evenly. Add three corn pieces and two cracked lobster claws to each bowl. Serve with hot corn tortillas and pass around the pepper sauce.

VENISON CHILI

Native Americans were cooking deer meat thousands of years ago. They had wild chiles and wild onions, but they didn't have skillets or garden vegetables. If you thought browning the meat and adding garlic and tomatoes was absolutely essential to making chili, give this simple recipe a try.

SERVES 2

2 cups water

1 teaspoon salt, plus more as needed

2 cups venison shoulder meat, cut in ½-inch cubes

2 tablespoons dried chiles (such as chile pequins)

2 green onions, chopped

In a saucepan over medium-high heat, bring the water and salt to a boil. Add the meat and ancho chile. Return to a boil, reduce the heat, and simmer for 40 minutes. Remove the ancho stem and the large pieces of ancho skin. Mash the softened ancho with a spoon and stir into the chili, mixing the chile and meat together. Add salt to taste. Serve garnished with chopped green onions.

FRESH CORN TORTILLAS

If you've ever watched a Latina grandma patting out handmade tortillas, you have a pretty good idea of the way that the Aztecs did it. The tortilla press, a contraption of two flat surfaces hinged together with a handle for pressing dough balls into flat circles, simplifies the task. I use circles cut from plastic shopping bags to keep the masa from sticking to the tortilla press. You can also use waxed paper. Fresh cooked tortillas are the ultimate accompaniment to a bowl of chili—or just about any Mexican dish. Put a fresh tortilla in one hand and a spoon in the other and let the taco happen.

MAKES 10 TORTILLAS

2 cups masa harina

¼ teaspoon salt

¼ teaspoon corn oil

Cut two 8-inch circles of plastic or waxed paper and set aside. Combine the masa harina with the salt and add water a tiny splash at a time, kneading the wet dough to incorporate more and more flour to make an elastic dough ball. Keep kneading and adding water until all of the flour has been incorporated. The dough should be flexible, not stiff. Cover with a damp towel and let rest for 10 minutes. Then form ten ping pong ball–size balls (2 ounces each).

Using a tortilla press, rolling pin, or the bottom of a pot, flatten each ball between the two sheets of plastic into a 5-inch tortilla.

Line a basket or bowl with a clean cloth napkin. Oil a *comal* or skillet with little corn oil and heat over high heat, until a drop of water sizzles. Hold a tortilla flat in the palm of your hand and flip your wrist to drop it flat onto the hot *comal*. Cook until the edges begin to harden and flecks of brown develop, about 2 minutes each side. Transfer to the basket and cover with the napkin to keep warm. Repeat until all the tortillas are cooked.

SMOKED TURKEY CHILI

Recipes that combine turkey and dried peppers predate the arrival of the Spanish and remain popular today. In her cookbook *Oaxaca al Gusto*, Diana Kennedy writes about a modern smoked turkey soup (*caldo de guajolote ahumado*) made with dried chiles and wild onions that is served with giant corn tortillas in the isolated mountains of the Yogope area. Here's a take on Mesoamerican turkey chili.

SERVES 6

2 smoked turkey legs

3 dried ancho chiles, stemmed and seeded

2 dried pasilla chiles, stemmed and seeded

1 dried guajillo chile or New Mexican long red chile

15 store-bought yellow corn tortillas

1½ pounds boneless skinless turkey breast, cut into ½-inch dice

1 onion, chopped

In a Dutch oven over medium-high heal, cover the turkey legs with water, bring to a boil, and reduce to a simmer. Cook for 2 to 3 hours, until the turkey meat is tender and slips easily from the bone, adding water as necessary. Clean the meat from the turkey bones and discard the skin and "quills." Chop the meat and reserve. Measure the broth and add water, if necessary, to equal 4 cups. Pour the broth back into the Dutch oven and bring to a boil, then reduce to a simmer.

Toast the chiles on a dry *comal* or skillet over high heat until slightly fragrant, then tear the chiles up, put them into a small saucepan, and add a cup or so of hot turkey broth. Simmer for a few minutes, until the chiles are no longer rigid, then turn off the heat and set aside to soften for at least 15 minutes. When the chiles are very soft, transfer them to a blender or food processor with the soaking liquid.

Toast nine of the tortillas on a dry *comal* or skillet over high heat until they are slightly charred. Reserve one tortilla for the garnish. Tear up the other eight tortillas and add them to the chiles and liquid in the blender. Puree until very smooth, at least 5 minutes.

Add the chile puree to the remaining broth in the Dutch oven and bring to a boil. Add the turkey breast meat and onion and cook until the turkey is done but still juicy, 7 to 10 minutes.

Heat the remaining six tortillas on a dry *comal* over medium heat, flipping them and shuffling until all are warmed and pliant. Cut the reserved tortilla into fine wisps. Divide the chili among six bowls and garnish with the tortilla wisps. Serve immediately with the hot tortillas.

CHAPTER 2

CHRISTMAS IN NEW MEXICO

The chile pepper is not just the heart and soul of New Mexico's cuisine, it is the totem of that state's culture.

"What'll it be?" the waitress at Santa Fe's Horseman's Haven Café asks me.

"Huevos rancheros," I say.

"Red or green?" she asks.

"Christmas," I respond, "over easy." This gets me a plate of fried eggs over a blue corn tortilla on a plate half covered in green chile sauce and half in red. I start with the roasted green chile sauce. The first few bites are frighteningly hot. I drink my coffee in one gulp and ask for some water. By the time I get to the red chile sauce, I am used to the heat, although I can't stop my nose from running.

The brick red sauce is made from Northern New Mexican red chile powder and a smattering of other ingredients. It looks and tastes sort of like Texas chili without the carne. But don't insult the locals by comparing New Mexican chile to what's called chili in the rest of the country.

New Mexicans were eating the dish we Americans call "chili" three hundred years ago. The first chile peppers cultivated in what is now the United States were planted by Juan de

Oñate's Mexican pioneers in 1609—by the 1700s, chile peppers were one of New Mexico's leading crops.

There are two chiles (one red, one green) on the signs that welcome you to "The Land of Enchantment" on the interstate highway—enchantment being synonymous with a good chile pepper buzz in these parts.

"Just like my mama used to make it," the Santa Fe cop seated beside me says with a smile as he watches me mop up the red chile sauce with a tortilla.

The only open seat at Horseman's Haven was at the counter. So I sat down beside Officer David de Baca. He was eating huevos rancheros with the restaurant's famously *picante* red chile sauce. At 8 a.m., the parking lot is packed with pick-up trucks, plumber's vans, contractor's vehicles, and police cars. There are seven booths and ten seats at the counter. Baca says he has been eating here two or three times a week since the place opened in 1978. The green chile is hot, he says, and the red is even hotter.

New Mexicans are annoyed that most of the country refers to their "long green chiles" as Anaheim peppers. That name was popularized by Emilio Ortega, a chile farmer who brought pepper seeds from New Mexico to Anaheim, California, in 1900. The canning company he founded grew into the giant Mexican food concern called Ortega. Chiles aren't even grown in Anaheim anymore. Meanwhile in New Mexico, two distinct chile cultures have emerged.

"What's the difference between chiles from northern New Mexico and the ones from the south?" I ask David de Baca.

"Down in Hatch, green chiles are going for maybe $15 a bushel," de Baca says. "Chimayó chiles are five times that price, if you can find them. I am going down to Hatch tomorrow to pick up a few bags. Then some friends and I will get together for a chile roasting party."

The valley of Chimayó is a little pocket of green tucked in between the red pipe organ cliffs and the pointy blue mountain peaks north of Santa Fe. There are people selling bags of red chile powder in the parking lot of El Sanctuario de Chimayó, the village's historic landmark.

"That's Hatch chile powder they're selling," scoffs a local chile farmer named Diego Ortiz, whom I stop to visit. "They sell it to tourists getting off the bus who don't know any better." We walk out to Ortiz's chile field, which looks to be about 1 acre. The bushes are around 2 feet high and are covered with twisted bullhorn-shaped chiles of 6 to 8 inches. This is the third and probably the last set of chiles that these plants will produce. The chiles are much smaller than the kind I am used to seeing.

"The Hatch chiles are big and thick, but they don't have any flavor. My son brought us a bag of those, but I threw them away," Ortiz says. The side of the barn beside the chile field is hung with dozens of long red chile *ristras*. Ortiz tells me the strings sell for $30 apiece. I try to buy one, but all of these have already been sold to the Rancho de Chimayó restaurant. I ask Ortiz why the Chimayó chile has become so rare and expensive.

"The labor is cheap down south. Up here, everything has gotten too expensive. Mexican laborers can't afford to live in Santa Fe. And farmland is all getting bought up."

There is a pile of chiles lying on the ground that have been rejected because they are broken. Ortiz picks one up, tears it, and tastes it. Then he gives me a chunk. The deep red chile flesh is extremely sweet and as flavorful as a good pimento. I pick up another one and tear off a piece. This one is as hot as a jalapeño.

"Wow, the heat levels are completely different," I remark.

"That's why we grind them all together into powder," Ortiz says. Ortiz will use the reject chiles for seed. "We have never bought seeds," he says. "I clean my own. These seeds go back to my father's chiles."

In Chimayó and the villages of the northern mountains, chiles are grown in small plots from seeds that have been saved from the previous year or bought from neighbors. The chiles are dried in *ristras* in the traditional manner and then ground into red chile powder. Chimayo chile powder is a rare treasure, and it's in very short supply.

"Don't even bother to tell people about Chimayó chile," says Florence Jaramillo, the owner of Rancho de Chimayó, when I sit down with her at the restaurant. "Nobody can get it anymore." Rancho de Chimayó uses about 5,000 pounds of green chiles and 5,000 pounds of red chiles every year. "I buy as much Chimayó as I can, but there is never enough. We have to buy Hatch chiles, too."

Chile peppers are New Mexico's number one cash food crop. In 2007, the value of New Mexico's chile pepper industry was estimated at more than $350 million. Scarce labor and a long drought have reduced the size of the chile crop by about a third in the last few years. Treasured for their flavor, New Mexican chiles are becoming more and more expensive.

Red chiles from Hatch are delicious. But the first time you taste beef cooked in a stew made with dark red Chimayó chile powder you have

to reconsider everything you thought you knew about chili. The rich, complex northern New Mexican red chiles makes the tastiest chili on the planet.

If they want to call it "chile" instead of chili, that's fine with me.

RED CHILE SAUCE

The colorful strings of red chiles called *ristras* seen hanging from the eaves of houses and barns all over New Mexico are used to make this red chile sauce. You can use whole red chiles, but it's more common to use crushed red chiles or red chile powder. Individual chiles from northern New Mexican chile-growing regions like Chimayó vary widely in heat level—combining lots of red chiles in one batch of powder makes for a more predictable flavor. Serve with huevos rancheros (page 42), as an enchilada sauce, or as a base for other recipes.

MAKES 6 CUPS

4 cups beef
or vegetable broth

4 New Mexican long
red chiles or guajillos,
or ¾ cup New Mexican
red chile powder

2 tomatoes, chopped,
or 1 cup crushed
canned tomatoes

2 teaspoons minced onion

1 teaspoon ground cumin

1 clove garlic, minced

1 teaspoon salt

½ teaspoon finely ground
black pepper

1 tablespoon
cornstarch dissolved in
2 tablespoons water

Combine the broth, chiles, tomatoes, onion, cumin, garlic, salt, and pepper in a saucepan. Bring to a boil over medium-high heat and reduce for 10 minutes. Add the cornstarch and reduce heat to a simmer. Cook until thickened, 5 to 10 more minutes, then use as desired.

RED CHILE CHORIZO

Homemade chorizo is worlds better than the store-bought stuff. It makes a fine breakfast taco with eggs or potatoes, and it's a great chili ingredient (see A. J. Foyt's SuperTex-Mex Chili, page 89). The red wine vinegar gives chorizo its distinctive flavor, so don't be tempted to leave out this key ingredient.

**MAKES 1 POUND UNCOOKED;
SERVES 10**

1 pound lean ground pork

2 teaspoons New Mexican red chile powder (see box on page 36), or substitute hot paprika

1 tablespoon sweet paprika

1 tablespoon salt

1 teaspoon garlic powder

1/2 teaspoon ground cumin

3 tablespoons
red wine vinegar

FOR COOKING

1 tablespoon peanut oil

2 tablespoons chopped onion

Combine the pork, chile powder, paprika, salt, garlic powder, cumin, and vinegar in a bowl and mix well with your hands. Store uncooked chorizo in the refrigerator for up to 4 days or the freezer for 3 months.

To cook 1 serving of chorizo, in a skillet or sauté pan over medium-high heat, heat the oil. Stir in the onion. Add 1/4 cup of the pork mixture and brown for 5 minutes, or to desired doneness. Mix with two scrambled eggs for a quick breakfast dish.

RED CHILE WITH BEEF

Eat a bowl of this full-flavored favorite and you'll understand what New Mexican chile and Texas chili have in common. Serve this as a stew with potato or corn added, or in a bowl with flour tortillas and beans on the side. Pass a garnish plate (see page 41) around the table.

SERVES 4

4 tablespoons peanut oil

1½ pounds beef chuck, cut into ½-inch dice

2 onions, chopped

3 cloves garlic, minced

6 cups Red Chile Sauce (page 32)

1 teaspoon salt

½ teaspoon finely ground black pepper

Water (optional)

1½ cups cooked potato chunks and/or corn kernels (optional)

Garnish Plate (page 41)

In a Dutch oven over medium-high heat, heat the oil. Add the meat and brown on all sides, about 5 minutes, then transfer to a plate. Add the onions and cook, stirring to scrape up any browned bits, until the onions begin to soften, about 3 minutes. Add the garlic and continue cooking until lightly browned. Add the Red Chile Sauce and stir to combine. Return the beef to the pot and simmer until the beef is tender, about 1 hour. Add water if needed to maintain a soupy consistency. Season to taste with salt and pepper then stir in the potato and corn and serve, passing the garnish plate at the table.

VARIATIONS

Red Chile with Venison Substitute 1½ pounds venison, lamb, or goat cut in ½-inch cubes and cook as directed above, until tender. Add corn or potatoes if desired and pass a garnish plate at the table.

Chile Colorado con Puerco Cut 1½ pounds lean pork into pencil-thin strips and brown as directed above, add 1 cup crushed tomatoes with the chile sauce, and simmer for 30 minutes, or until tender. Add corn or potatoes if desired and pass a garnish plate at the table.

Red Chile with Turkey and Beans Substitute 1½ pounds ground turkey for the beef, add cooked white beans or garbanzo beans (page 121) with the chile sauce, and simmer for 20 minutes or until well-cooked. Pass a garnish plate at the table.

CONTINUED

Red Chile Posole Make as above, but instead of corn or potatoes, add 3½ cups drained fresh-cooked hominy or 1 (30-ounce) can of white hominy, drained and rinsed, with the red chile sauce. Pass a garnish plate at the table.

WHERE TO BUY RED CHILE POWDER

Bueno Foods of Albuquerque sells New Mexican long red and green chiles in a variety of forms and red chile powder in several heat levels. Bueno's Special Reserve Premium Red Chile Powder is the best red chile powder I have found on the national mail-order market.

HATCH GREEN CHILE SAUCE

If you live in a part of the country where green chiles are roasted outdoors in the late summer and early fall, plan to buy a whole bag and then freeze the roasted chiles in individual packages. A pound and a half of whole roasted green chiles yields about one pound (2 cups) after the skins and stems are removed. Don't bother removing the seeds—these chiles aren't very hot anyway. To roast green chiles at home, see the recipe on page 19.

Serve green chile sauce with huevos rancheros (page 42) or vegetables, or as an enchilada sauce.

MAKES 6 CUPS

1 pound tomatillos (5 to 8), husked and rinsed

4 cups vegetable broth

2 cups chopped roasted New Mexican long green chiles or Anaheim chiles (see page 19)

2 teaspoons minced onion

½ teaspoon dried Mexican oregano

1 clove garlic, minced

½ teaspoon salt

¼ teaspoon white pepper

1 tablespoon cornstarch dissolved in 2 tablespoons water (optional)

Cover the tomatillos with water in a saucepan, cover, and bring to a boil. Remove the lid, reduce the heat, and simmer until they become softened and dull in color, about 15 minutes. Drain the tomatillos and transfer them to a food processor, then puree. Combine the broth, roasted chiles, pureed tomatillos, onion, oregano, garlic, salt, and white pepper in a saucepan. Bring to a boil over medium-high heat and reduce for 10 minutes. Add the cornstarch mixture, reduce the heat to a simmer, and cook until thickened, 5 to 10 more minutes. Add water to equal 6 cups of sauce, then serve as desired.

GREEN CHILE CHICKEN

Here's an amazingly simple chicken and chile dinner that's ready fast and is extremely tasty.

SERVES 4

2 pounds boneless,
skinless chicken breasts

4 cups Hatch Green Chile
Sauce (page 37)

½ cup crumbled
cotija cheese

Garnish plate (see page 41)

Flour tortillas, to serve

Preheat the oven to 350°F.

Arrange the chicken in a single layer an ovenproof casserole that can double as a serving dish. Pour the sauce over the chicken and bake until the sauce bubbles and the chicken is cooked through, 25 to 35 minutes. (The USDA recommends cooking chicken to an internal temperature of 165°F.)

Remove the dish from the oven and crumble the cheese over the chicken. Pass the garnish plate at the table and serve with flour tortillas.

GREEN CHILE WITH PORK AND POTATOES

This is the classic green chile stew. Garbanzo beans (also known as chickpeas) are also a popular addition. Serve with warm flour tortillas and beans.

SERVES 4

2 pounds boneless pork loin chops

2 thick-cut strips bacon, finely chopped

2 onions, chopped

3 cloves garlic, minced

2 to 3 serrano chiles, minced (optional)

6 cups Hatch Green Chile Sauce (page 37)

2 cups diced cooked potatoes

Trim the pork chops and discard the fat; cut the meat into pencil-thin slices 1½ inches long. You should get 1¾ pounds of meat.

Heat a Dutch oven over medium-high heat and render the bacon, stirring often. When the bacon has given up its grease (this should take about 3 minutes), add the pork and brown, turning on all sides, for about 7 minutes. Add the onions and scrape up any browned bits on the bottom of the pot. Add the garlic and the serrano and cook for another 3 minutes. Add the green chile sauce, bring to a boil, and reduce to a simmer. Cook until the pork is tender, about 30 minutes.

Add the potatoes and enough water to keep the stew at the desired consistency and cook until the potatoes are heated through, then serve.

VARIATIONS

Green Chile Posole Add 1 teaspoon cumin and ½ teaspoon dried Mexican oregano with the garlic, and substitute 3½ cups drained fresh-cooked hominy or 1 (30-ounce) can of white hominy, drained and rinsed, for the potatoes. Serve with a garnish plate (see below).

Green Chile with Turkey Substitute ground turkey for the pork and simmer for 20 minutes, or until well-cooked.

GARNISH PLATE

When serving red or green chile stew or posole, a plate of condiments is served on the side or a larger plate is passed around the table.

For each person, you will need: ¼ cup chopped onion, ¼ cup chopped fresh cilantro, 1 teaspoon minced serrano. For posole or other soups, add: 2 lime wedges, 2 sliced radishes, 1 cup shaved raw cabbage.

HUEVOS RANCHEROS "CHRISTMAS"

You can make New Mexican–style huevos rancheros with either red chile sauce or green chile sauce, but I like "Christmas" (red and green side by side). The eggs taste best on a freshly fried corn tortilla with lots of refried beans. Cotija cheese (*queso anejo*) is a crumbly cow's milk cheese available in Mexican markets, but if you can't find any, substitute a mild feta.

SERVES 4

Corn oil

4 corn tortillas, homemade (page 25) or store-bought

2 cups Frijoles Refritos (page 81)

2 cups Red Chile Sauce (page 32)

2 cups Hatch Green Chile Sauce (page 37)

Butter

8 eggs

Salt and finely ground black pepper

1 cup chopped tomatoes, to garnish

4 teaspoons fresh chopped cilantro, to garnish

1 cup cotija cheese

Preheat the oven to its lowest setting. Put four dinner plates in the oven to warm.

Heat ½ inch corn oil in a small skillet over medium-high heat until a tortilla dipped in the oil sizzles. Use tongs to dip one tortilla into the oil, turning until it is slightly crisp on both sides, about 1 minute. Put the freshly fried tortilla in a baking dish in the oven. Repeat with the remaining tortillas. Warm the chile sauces and refried beans in saucepans or in the microwave.

Put a ½-cup dollop of refried beans in the middle of each of four warmed plates. Spread ½ cup of red chile sauce on one side of the plate and ½ cup green chile sauce on the other. Repeat with all four plates. Lower a fried tortilla into place in the center of each plate, using the refried beans as "glue."

In an egg pan or skillet, heat enough butter to cover the bottom. Fry the eggs, two at a time, sunny-side up or over easy, for about 4 minutes total. Repeat heating butter and cooking eggs two at a time until all of them are cooked.

To serve, slide two eggs onto each tortilla, season with salt and pepper, and garnish with the tomatoes, cilantro, and cotija cheese. Carry the plates to the table carefully so that the sauces remain separate.

CHAPTER 3
GOULASH, KIMA, AND TAGINE

Gulyás means "cowboy" in Hungarian. When you say *Gulasch* in German or goulash in English, you are talking about a Hungarian "cowboy soup." The dish is named after the cowboys who first prepared it while they herded cattle on the Great Hungarian Plain, or Puszta, in the nineteenth century.

I learned about the Hungarian cowboys and their peppery soup during a summer vacation. My wife set up a home exchange with a family in Leipzig, Germany, and we took a side trip to Prague. In Prague's Old Town, I ate a spectacular venison goulash with Carlsbad dumplings at a cozy inn by the river. There was another goulash presented in a hollowed-out bread bowl, and a third rich brick-red beef goulash puddle served on a plate with bread dumplings at a traditional Czech restaurant near the Tower. The variations were endless.

German immigrant William Gebhardt made chili powder famous.

"You eat goulash at every meal?" asked Reingard Klingler, a family friend from Vienna who had joined us for a weekend during our vacation. When I told her I was exploring the cultural connection between Central European goulash and Texas chili, she was intrigued. And as I explained to Reingard, goulash turned out to have more in common with Texas chili than I ever imagined.

Besides the fact that Hungarian *gulyás* and Texas chili are both associated with cowboy cultures and both were originally made on cattle drives with beef, peppers, and very little else, they were made in similar pots. The heavy cast-iron pot called a *bogrács* in Hungarian is set directly over hot coals, just like the cast-iron Dutch oven of American cowboy chuck wagons.

Perhaps the two cowboy cultures developed similar dishes by coincidence. But the one unmistakable influence that Hungarian goulash had on American-style chili came in a tin of paprika. In 1884, a man named Janos Kotányi introduced his signature paprika powder to Austrian markets—the first mass-produced pepper powder to be sold commercially. "Kotányi is still the most famous brand in Vienna," my friend Reingard told me. Mass-produced Hungarian paprika powder made it possible to prepare goulash and other such dishes far from the Hungarian pepper fields.

Kotányi's Hungarian paprika powder inspired a young German immigrant named William Gebhardt to use his home oven and an imported hand-cranked coffee mill—a standard item in German households of the era in Texas—to create an ancho chili powder that he named "Tampico Dust." For several years, beginning in 1895, Gebhardt sold his little glass bottles in the streets of San Antonio—he could only make four cases at a time—but that would soon change.

Gebhardt's Eagle Brand Chili Powder, a proprietary blend of ancho chile powder, cumin, and oregano, was patented in 1899. The shelf-stable instant mix standardized the flavor of chili con carne across the country.

Born in Germany in 1875, William Gebhardt immigrated to the German town of New Braunfels just north of San Antonio in 1883. In 1892, the young Gebhardt opened a café at the back of a popular local saloon. His specialty was chili, which was familiar to the German population of New Braunfels both because

of the proximity of the Mexican-American cooking of San Antonio (more on that in the Chili Queens chapter, page 67), and because it so closely resembled German *gulasch*.

At the time, chili was made with whole dried ancho chiles imported from San Luis Potosi, Mexico. To stock up for a whole year required a wagonload of dried chiles. The supply was seasonal, and the dried chiles were often spoiled by moisture or insects during the long months of storage.

Over time, Gebhardt expanded his company into one of the largest spice manufacturing concerns in the world and added a cannery to produce canned chili, canned tamales, and canned beans.

Skeptics of the goulash-chili connection will want to take a look at the first Gebhardt cookbook, published in 1908. It included a recipe for authentic goulash using Gebhardt chili powder instead of Hungarian paprika along with an American goulash recipe that is still popular in the German communities of the Texas Hill Country.

Many chili powders on the American market contain paprika, which means the border between chili and goulash remains a fine line, even today. Granted, a bowl of goulash is typically milder and sweeter than a bowl of chili—but authentic Hungarian goulash can be quite spicy and American chili can be very mild. Reingard tells me, "My friends and I love hot and spicy food. We make goulash at home in

Delicious Mexican Dishes easily made with

Gebhardt's Chili Con Carne

PLAIN
WITHOUT BEANS

Made by the original recipe, of choicest cuts of Government-inspected beef, cooked to juicy tenderness and flavored with Ancho chili peppers and blended native spices. Covered with savory, red brown gravy. Cooked without beans to retain the true meaty flavor of the Mexican dish.

Delicious served plain or with Gebhardt's Mexican Style Beans. See recipes for dishes easily made with plain Chili con Carne as a base.

« 10 »

BEEF À LA MODE

No. 2 can Gebhardt's Plain Chili con Carne	½ c. potatoes, diced
1 qt. water	½ c. turnips, diced
No. 1 can tomatoes	½ c. celery, diced
½ c. carrots, diced	1 onion, chopped
	2 t. salt

Using a large, deep pot cook the vegetables in the boiling salted water about 10 minutes; add the contents of a can of Gebhardt's Plain Chili con Carne, a can of tomatoes and simmer until the vegetables are tender and gravy is heavy. Do not over-cook the vegetables for as soon as the vegetables lose their identity, the attractiveness of any dish is lost.

MEXICAN STEW

1 qt. salted water	1 onion, sliced
1 c. carrots, diced	No. 1 Gebhardt's Plain Chili con Carne
1 c. potatoes, diced	

Cook vegetables in salted water about 10 minutes; add contents of No. 1 can of Gebhardt's Plain Chili con Carne and simmer until vegetables are tender and gravy is heavy.

GEBHARDT'S TAMALES WITH CHILI

| No. 2 can Gebhardt's Real Mexican Tamales | No. 1 Gebhardt's Plain Chili con Carne |

Heat Tamales and Plain Chili con Carne in cans. Arrange Tamales parallel to each other on hot platter and pour over Chili con Carne. Serve with dill pickles.

CHILI AND RICE CONES

1 c. rice	No. 1 can Gebhardt's Plain Chili con Carne
½ t. salt	
3 c. water	

Steam the rice in the salted water until tender. Mold into cones

and pour over the hot Gebhardt's Plain Chili con Carne. Garnish with sour chunk pickles and sprigs of parsley. Serve at once.

» 11 »

Vienna that is much hotter than the restaurant stuff. But we usually just start with sweet paprika and doctor it up with cayenne and hot sauce." The most notable difference between the flavor signatures of chili and goulash are in the aromatics of cumin seeds versus caraway seeds. In German, caraway is known as *echter Kümmel* and cumin is *Kreuzkümmel*. So you might say it all comes down to the *Kümmel*.

Like the venison goulash I ate in Prague, the versions of goulash served in Central European restaurants get very elaborate. I read a magazine article that described the goulash served by half a dozen famous Prague chefs.

The recipes included one made with several cuts of beef including beef heart, an all-pork version, and a vegan goulash. It seems the more expensive the restaurant, the more ingredients in the goulash.

After visiting Prague, I returned to our borrowed house in Leipzig, eager to experiment with goulash recipes. I went on a paprika-buying spree in Leipzig supermarkets where I marveled at my choices of grades, brands, and heat levels. I bought hot (*sharf*) paprika, sweet paprika, a "goulash blend" that contained "*Kümmel*," and a small package of exotic "*rosen*" paprika.

I cooked a creamy chicken paprikash with sweet paprika that the kids loved, a fiery beef goulash with *sharf* paprika that tasted nearly identical to New Mexican Red Chile with Beef (page 35), a pork goulash, and a famous variation of pork goulash with sauerkraut and sour cream.

One day, while driving through Leipzig's industrial district, I noticed a food stand called Gulaschcanone Leipzig. The menu, which was painted on the outside wall so you could read it while stopped at the traffic light advertised "chili con carne." I pulled the car over and checked it out.

In a parking lot, there were some picnic tables outside of a large tent that held the food stall. Parked halfway in and halfway out of the tent was an unusual-looking Army surplus trailer with a wood-fired stove that heated three huge covered kettles. The olive drab–painted trailer had large wheels so it could be pulled behind a military truck just like an artillery piece. German soldiers nicknamed this kind of mobile kitchen a *Gulaschcanone*, or "goulash cannon," hence the name of the food stall.

Gulaschcanone Leipzig was owned by a young entrepreneur named Ken Weber; it had been in operation since 2006. The rotating menu included *Erbseneintopf mit Kasseler* (pea soup with ham), *Soljanka* (Eastern European sour and spicy soup), and chili con carne.

Surprisingly, the one thing Ken Weber never cooked in his goulash cannon was goulash.

Everybody and their grandma cooks goulash in Germany—chili con carne sounds much more exotic.

GOULASH DOGMA

Like chili cook-off competitors, goulash aficionados are quite vehement in their opinions and proud of their recipes. The famous Hungarian food writer and Budapest restaurant owner, George Lang, gives these commandments to would-be goulash makers:

Never use any flour.

Never use any other spice besides caraway.

Never Frenchify it with wine.

Never Germanize it with brown sauce.

Like a pot of old-fashioned Texas chili, the essential Hungarian goulash is very simple. If you love chili, odds are you will have a lot of fun with the authentic goulash recipes in the following pages.

You'll also find recipes for the other international chilis that undoubtedly influenced our American version. There's a Berber tagine that illustrates the influence of cumin in chili con carne. There's a Pakistani keema that will remind you that spicy ground meat mixtures have been popular in world cuisines for a long time. And last but not least, there's the recipe for Greek Makaronia me Kima, the inspiration for Cincinnati chili (see page 123).

PAPRIKA VARIETIES

Peppers were introduced to Hungary by the Ottoman Turks in the sixteenth century. Paprika peppers were hybridized and improved over the centuries. But the fame of Hungarian paprika declined under Communism, when quality was sacrificed for quantity. Paprika from Spain and other countries took over the market.

Paprika had gotten sweeter and sweeter over the years, as chefs and European gourmets traditionally considered the mildest to be the most elegant. But recently, hot and spicy flavors have become more popular all over the world, especially among younger people, and hot paprika is gaining in popularity.

Smoked paprika (*pimentón*) and hot paprika are now widely available in the United States along with several brands of Hungarian paprika.

Recently, entrepreneurs and small farmers have started reviving the Hungarian paprika industry with heirloom pepper varieties and more careful small-batch processing. In Central Europe, shoppers have as many as eight different "grades" of paprika to choose from.

The "exquisite" grades are considered the highest quality, but the hotter varieties are in demand, too. Most paprika varieties are available by mail order from Internet sources.

HUNGARIAN PAPRIKA GRADES

Noble Sweet (*édesnemes*): Slightly pungent and bright red, this is the grade of Hungarian paprika most widely available in the United States.

Half-Sweet (*félédes*): A blend of mild and hot paprika.

Strong (*erős*): The hottest paprika, light brown or orange-ish in color.

Special quality (*különleges*): Mild and very sweet with a bright red color.

Delicate (*csípősmentes csemege*): A mild paprika with a rich flavor and darker red color.

Exquisite Delicate (*csemegepaprika*): Hotter version of Delicate.

Pungent Exquisite Delicate (*csípős csemege, pikáns*): An even hotter version of Delicate.

Rose (*rózsa*): Pale red in color with a strong aroma and medium heat.

SPICY HUNGARIAN GOULASH

Sweet Hungarian paprika is widely available in the United States. It is also increasingly common to find Hungarian hot paprika and several varieties of Spanish paprika in gourmet food stores. (Smoked paprika, or *pimentón*, is not recommended for goulash.) But paprika connoisseurs may want to order their spices on the Internet, where an astounding selection of paprika varieties are available (see page 49). Goulash tastes better reheated the next day and also freezes well, for up to 2 months. Serve over wide egg noodles.

SERVES 4

1 pound beef stew meat

Salt and finely ground black pepper

4 onions

2 plum tomatoes

1 red pepper (Hungarian paprika pepper or other thick-skinned red pepper preferred)

3 tablespoons peanut oil

¼ cup hot Hungarian paprika

1 cup water, plus more as needed

Sour cream, for serving

Chopped fresh parsley, for serving

Cut the beef into ½-inch dice, removing any obvious ligaments and season with salt and pepper. Halve the onions vertically and slice from end to end into crescent-shaped slivers. Chop the tomatoes and red pepper, keeping each separate.

Heat 1½ tablespoons of the oil in a Dutch oven over medium heat and fry the onions, stirring occasionally until soft and golden in color, 15 to 20 minutes. At the same time, heat the remaining 1½ tablespoons oil in a skillet over medium-high heat and brown the meat in small batches. Transfer each batch of cooked beef onto a plate.

When the onions are soft and golden, add the paprika, stirring well to combine. Add the meat, the chopped tomatoes, and red pepper and stir together. Deglaze the skillet in which the meat was cooked with 1 cup of water, scraping up the brown bits on the bottom, and add to the onion mixture.

Simmer, covered, checking often to make sure the stew doesn't stick to the pan, until the meat is fork tender and the vegetables begin to dissolve into a thick sauce, about 1 hour, adding water as necessary. Serve topped with sour cream and parsley.

GOULASH CANNON CHILI

This is the recipe I got from Ken Weber, the owner of the Goulash Cannon food stand in Leipzig, Germany—it tastes a lot better than it sounds! Sambal olek is a thick red Indonesian pepper paste and can be found on the international aisle of the supermarket.

SERVES 4

2 tablespoons peanut oil

2 pounds ground beef

1 (28-ounce) can diced tomatoes

1 (6-ounce) can tomato paste

2 cloves garlic, minced

¼ cup plus 1 tablespoon sambal olek

1 (15-ounce) can red kidney beans, drained and rinsed

1 (15-ounce) can white kidney beans, drained and rinsed

Chopped onion, for garnish

Shredded Gouda, for garnish

Heat the olive oil in a Dutch oven over medium-high heat. Add the beef and cook until browned, 5 to 7 minutes. Add the diced tomatoes, tomato paste, garlic, sambal olek, red kidney beans, and white kidney beans. Simmer 30 minutes or until flavors mellow. Divide into 4 bowls and garnish with the onions and cheese.

PORK GOULASH

Pork chunks for goulash are sold pre-packaged in European supermarkets—but you can make your pork goulash with boneless pork chops. Avoid pork shoulder cuts because they contain too much cartilage.

SERVES 4

1 pound boneless pork, cut into ½-inch dice, cartilage removed

Salt and freshly ground black pepper

4 onions

4 strips bacon, chopped

¼ cup Hungarian sweet paprika

1 teaspoon caraway seeds

1 clove garlic, minced

1 red bell pepper, chopped

1½ cups tomato puree

2 cups chicken broth

1 tablespoon brown sugar

Freshly cooked egg noodles, to serve

Season the pork with salt and pepper. Halve the onions vertically and slice from end to end into crescent-shaped slivers.

Cook half the bacon in a Dutch oven over medium-high heat until the fat is rendered; remove the bacon and reserve. Reduce the heat to medium, add the onions and sauté in the bacon drippings until soft and golden in color, 15 to 20 minutes. At the same time, add the remaining bacon to a skillet over medium-high heat and render the fat. Remove the bacon and reserve. Brown the pork in small batches in the rendered bacon drippings until browned, about 5 minutes. Transfer each batch of cooked meat to a plate along with the bacon.

When the onions are soft and golden, add the paprika and caraway seeds, stirring well to combine. Add the pork, the garlic, bell pepper, and tomato puree, stir together. Deglaze the skillet in which the meat was cooked with the chicken stock, scraping up the brown bits on the bottom. Add the stock and brown sugar to the onion mixture.

Simmer, covered, checking often to make sure the stew doesn't stick to the pan. Continue simmering until the meat is tender and the vegetables dissolve into a thick sauce, adding water as necessary to prevent sticking. Serve over noodles, garnished with crispy bacon.

VARIATION

Pork Goulash with Sauerkraut (*Székelygulyás* in Hungary and *Tsegediner Gulasch* in Austria): Combine 1 cup sour cream with 1 cup heavy cream, add 1 teaspoon of flour and mix until well blended. Stir half of the cream mixture and 1 pound drained, fresh-pack sauerkraut into the goulash when it is nearly finished. Put the rest of the sour cream mixture in a bowl and pass around the table.

CHICKEN PAPRIKASH

Peppers, onions, and hot paprika slowly simmered with meat make this Hungarian chicken dish very similar to chicken chili. You can make this dish very mild with *csípősmentes csemege* (sweet paprika), medium hot with *félédes* paprika, or blistering hot with fiery *erős* paprika. If you are using the standard *édesnemes* paprika usually found in America, you make the dish spicy by adding some cayenne. Serve over rice, spaetzle, egg noodles, or potatoes.

SERVES 6 TO 8

3½ pounds whole chicken

Salt and freshly ground black pepper

2 to 3 large yellow onions

Butter (optional)

1 red pepper (preferably Hungarian paprika or other thick-skinned red pepper), cut into 1-inch dice

3 tablespoons sweet Hungarian paprika

1 teaspoon hot paprika or cayenne pepper, or to taste

½ cup sour cream

Cut off the wing tips from the chicken. Cut the backbone out of the chicken and place the back and wing segments in a stockpot with enough water to cover. Bring to a boil, reduce to a simmer, and cook for 20 minutes, or until the broth is nicely flavored.

Remove the yellow fat and the tail segment from the chicken and render in a Dutch oven over medium-low heat until the schmaltz is released, about 5 minutes.

Cut the chicken into pieces. (It doesn't matter how many; the chicken will eventually be removed from the bones and chopped.) Season the chicken pieces with salt and pepper and let them sit at room temperature while you prepare the onions. Cut off the ends and remove the skins from the onions and throw the trimmings into the stock pot. Halve the onions vertically and slice from end to end to make crescent-shaped slivers.

Place the chicken pieces skin-side down in the hot schmaltz, adding a little butter if needed to keep each piece of chicken coated. Let the chicken pieces cook until well browned on one side, 4 to 5 minutes; then turn them over and let them cook for 2 to 3 minutes on the other side until browned. Remove the chicken from the Dutch oven and set aside.

CONTINUED

Add the sliced onions and red pepper to the Dutch oven and cook over low heat, stirring occasionally and scraping up the browned bits from the chicken. Simmer over very low heat while the chicken stock is cooking.

Add the paprikas and some black pepper to the onions and stir to combine. Strain the broth and add 1½ cups to the pan, again scraping up the browned bits from the bottom of the pan. Nestle the chicken pieces into the pan with the onions.

Cover and cook over a low simmer until the chicken is cooked through, about 30 minutes. (If you like it well done, the chicken begins to fall off the bone after about 45 minutes.) When the chicken is done to your liking, remove from the pot and allow to cool. When the pan has cooled, slowly stir in the sour cream and add salt to taste. Add more stock if the sauce is too thick. If the sour cream cools the sauce too much, turn the heat back on just enough to warm it through—but do not bring to a boil.

Remove the chicken from the bone, discard the skin and bones and mix the chicken into the sauce. Serve immediately.

GREEK MAKARONIA ME KIMA

Cincinnati's Greek immigrants brought another dish to America that became part of the chili tradition. *Kima* is a spicy meat stew that is traditionally eaten with spaghetti. The Italian word *macaroni* comes from the Greek *makaronia*, which literally means "food made from barley." In both languages, the word refers to all types of pasta. Here's a recipe for the original Greek dish before it was Americanized.

SERVES 4 TO 6

½ cup olive oil

2 white onions, chopped

2 cloves garlic, chopped

1 pound lean ground beef

2 cups canned peeled plum tomatoes, with juice

½ cup red wine, Mavrodaphne preferred

1 medium cinnamon stick, broken in half

3 allspice berries

2 whole cloves

2 bay leaves, crumbled

10 black peppercorns

Pinch of nutmeg

Pinch of dried oregano

Water (optional)

Salt

1 pound spaghetti, prepared per package instructions

Mizithra cheese (or other dry cheese, such as queso fresco), shredded

In a large skillet or pot, heat the oil over medium heat. Add the onions, garlic, and meat and sauté, breaking up the meat with the side of a wooden spoon or spatula, until lightly colored, 5 to 7 minutes. Add the tomatoes and their juice, wine, cinnamon, allspice berries, cloves, bay leaves, peppercorns, nutmeg, and oregano, stirring well. Decrease the heat to a simmer, cover, and simmer for about 1 hour, until the meat has broken down and is tender. Add water, if needed, to prevent the sauce from burning. As the sauce cooks, skim off any fat that forms on the surface, if desired.

Add salt to taste. Serve on a bed of spaghetti, topped with mizithra or other shredded cheese.

CINCINNATI CHILI ORIGINS

To escape persecution and the threat of military conscription during World War I, Slavic Macedonians like the Kiradjieff family, who opened Cincinnati's first chili parlor in the 1920s, immigrated from what is now Northern Greece to the United States. Macedonian immigrants opened most of Cincinnati's early chili parlors and their descendants are still running some of them today.

Originally located near movie theaters, chili parlors offered families an inexpensive alternative to formal restaurants. Today, there are hundreds of chili parlors in Cincinnati, and the category keeps growing (see page 123).

MELTING POT CHILI

The unique, cumin-heavy flavor signature of Texas chili con carne was probably introduced by immigrants from the Canary Islands in the early 1700s.

Bexar, as San Antonio was once known, had very few residents, so the government of New Spain recruited settlers from the Spanish-held islands off the coast of North Africa. In March of 1731, fifteen families from the Canary Islands established the village now called "La Villita" not far from the Alamo. The families and their offspring supplied the community with most of its leaders for many years.

The primary inhabitants of the Canary Islands were the Guanches, a Berber people. Their cuisine contained lots of cumin, garlic, and chiles—as do most cuisines of Arab Africa. In San Antonio, the women from the Canary Islands reportedly made a "spicy stew" that was cooked outdoors in copper kettles in the village plaza and shared with soldiers and passersby at sundown.

It has been mistakenly suggested that the Canary Islanders brought cumin to Texas. In fact, *comino* can be found on mission shipping lists of the 1700s, so we know it was already there. What the Canary Islanders more likely introduced was a propensity to use cumin in larger quantities than the Spanish.

Canary Islanders owned extensive cattle herds of their own, so beef was plentiful and cheap.

The "spicy stew" the Canary Island women reportedly prepared probably resembled a Morrocan tagine or keema. Tagine is a stew containing large chunks of meat and made in a distinctive cone-shaped pot. Keema is a spicy minced meat dish typically made with goat or lamb. Both are seasoned with chiles, cumin, coriander, and garlic.

Keema is originally of Central Asian origin—the name describes a variety of spicy minced meat dishes common throughout South Asia, North Africa, and the Middle East. Spellings include *qeema* in India, *kiyma* in Turkey, *gheymah* in Armenia—and *kima* in Greece. Greek kima was the inspiration for Cincinnati chili.

But immigrants haven't just influenced the flavors of various American chili styles, they've also shaped America chili culture. The women from the Canary Islands introduced outdoor socializing around the stewpot to San Antonio, a tradition that inspired the legendary Chili Queens (see page 69).

And the multicultural evolution of chili is still going on. Pakistani immigrants in Houston prepare keema with beef because it's so much cheaper than goat or lamb. And they serve it with whole wheat flour tortillas, which look and taste just like the Indian flatbread called chapati.

Roll up your Mexican chapati with some keema and seasoned onions inside, and you've got yourself a Pakistani chili taco.

Descendants of Canary Islanders laying flowers on an outdoor altar on the doorstep of the Spanish Govenor's Palace, San Antonio, 1933

BERBER TAGINE

The cumin, chile, and garlic flavor signature of American chili is also common to Berber tagines and Moroccan stews. This traditional Moroccan "bachelor stew" made of meat chunks, onions, and a spice mix that includes chile powder (paprika) and cumin might be similar to the stews the Canary Islanders brought to San Antonio in the early 1700s. Serve over rice or with flatbread.

SERVES 4

2 cloves garlic, minced

1 teaspoon ground cumin

½ teaspoon hot Hungarian paprika

½ teaspoon freshly ground black pepper

½ teaspoon ground turmeric

½ teaspoon ground ginger

½ teaspoon salt

1½ pounds boneless leg of lamb, with fat removed, flesh cut into ½-inch dice

2 large yellow onions, quartered

½ cup beef broth

Preheat the oven to 350°F. Combine the garlic, cumin, paprika, pepper, turmeric, ginger, and salt in a bowl. Add the meat and toss until well coated.

Lay the onion quarters in the bottom of a tagine or 8-inch square baking dish and add the broth. Put the meat on top of the onions. Bake covered for 2½ to 3 hours until the meat is tender, then serve.

INDIAN/PAKISTANI KEEMA

"Black salt" or *kala namak*, a pink or purple rock salt extracted from the Himalayas, is a traditional ingredient that lends a unique, slightly sulfurous flavor to the chili. Black cardamom is larger and more complex than common green cardamom. Black salt, cardamom, and the prepared ginger/garlic paste called for here are available at Indian and Pakistani grocery stores.

SERVES 4

¼ cup peanut oil

2½ onions, finely chopped

6 whole black peppercorns

6 whole cloves

2 black cardamom pods

½ teaspoon whole cumin seeds

2 teaspoons ground coriander

1 teaspoons salt,
or more to taste

½ teaspoon black salt

½ teaspoon ground turmeric

1 teaspoon hot dried Kashmiri chilli powder (or substitute hot paprika or cayenne pepper)

1½ teaspoons ginger paste

1½ teaspoons garlic paste

3 tablespoons yogurt

3 ripe tomatoes, chopped

1 pound lean ground beef

2¼ cups water

Mashed potatoes, to serve

Chopped cilantro and raw onion, to serve

Heat the oil in a large pot or skillet over medium-high heat, add 2 of the onions, and cook until softened and translucent, about 5 minutes. Add the peppercorns, cloves, cardamom, cumin seeds, coriander, salt, "black salt," turmeric, chilli powder, ginger paste, and garlic paste and continue cooking for 2 minutes, stirring constantly to prevent burning. Add the yogurt and chopped tomatoes. Cook over medium heat until the liquid has evaporated and the mixture is almost dry again, about 8 minutes. Add the ground beef and ¼ cup of the water and increase the heat to high, stirring as needed to keep the mixture from burning, until the liquid has almost evaporated, about 10 minutes. Add the remaining 2 cups of water, reduce the heat to medium, and simmer until the water has evaporated, about 15 minutes. Taste and adjust salt if required. Spread mashed potatoes on a serving plate and top with the keema, garnish with chopped onions and cilantro, and serve immediately.

TEX-MEX TRADITIONS

CHAPTER 4

LONGHORNS, CHILI QUEENS, AND THE CRADLE OF TEXAS CHILI

Longhorn beef was so tough, it was barely edible. In the Spanish missions of the early 1700s, cattle were raised for other purposes. Each mission had a ranch in the remote plains where cattle, goats, and sheep were tended by vaqueros. While they were herding cattle, the vaqueros ate cabrito, small goats that provided just enough meat for a few cowboys. The cattle were driven to the mission a few at a time and slaughtered when needed.

Hides and the beef fat called tallow were the most profitable products longhorn cattle provided. The hides were cured for leather to make saddles, reins, whips, boots, belts, rawhide ropes, and other necessities. The tallow was used as a fuel and to make candles and soap. It was also a handy cooking fat. Hides and tallow could be shipped long distances, so they were often exported.

Early Tejano vaqueros

Of course, the stringy beef wasn't discarded. Chopping it into tiny pieces and simmering it in tallow was one of the only ways to make it palatable. The addition of spicy dried chile peppers provided flavor and helped preserve the stew.

Today we skim our chili carefully to remove any trace of grease. But in the days of the vaqueros, the spicy orange grease that rose to the top of the pot was a treasured part of the dish—old-time cowboys dipped their crackers or tortillas in it. The sauce called chili gravy (see page 77) was originally made with this orange grease.

The custom of eating chili with lots of grease hasn't entirely died out. In several chili parlors I visited as I traveled across the country, I found "wet" versions of chili that intentionally included lots of molten beef fat, or "chili juice." At the Hard Times chili chain in the Washington, DC, area, you order Texas chili wet, medium, or dry—based on how much melted tallow you want.

But wherever I went, I discovered that the oldest recipes for chili had something in common—they all started with the savory trinity of beef, suet, and chili powder.

SUET AND TALLOW

Suet is the raw (unrendered) fat from the kidney area of a side of beef; it is often called for in traditional British recipes for puddings and suet dumplings. (It also makes a nice pie crust.) Some old Texas chili recipes called for lean beef and suet to be ground up together—others called for rendering the suet and browning the meat in it.

Rendered beef fat (and lamb fat) is called tallow. Beef tallow can be made from suet or from the hard fat trimmed from other beef cuts. Along with lard, tallow was once among America's most common cooking fats. Because of its superior flavor, McDonald's used to cook its French fries in tallow. Outback Steakhouse still uses tallow to fry their tasty "blooming onion." Suet and other forms of beef fat are extremely inexpensive—if you can find them.

When I asked the butcher at my local grocery store for beef fat, he told me he would save the fat after cutting steaks and roasts the next morning. When I got there the next day, he handed me about 4 pounds of pure white suet and 4 pounds of flat pieces of beef back fat with streaks of lean. He charged me $1.79 a pound. I kept the suet separate and used it for recipes that called for unrendered suet. See the box at right for my method for rendering the beef fat.

RENDERED TALLOW

If you refrigerate the beef fat, it is easier to run through a meat grinder. Melting the ground fat in a slow oven takes longer, but avoids splatters on the stovetop.

MAKES 2½ POUNDS (3¾ CUPS)

4 pounds chilled beef fat

Preheat the oven to 250°F. Grind the fat in a meat grinder into a coarse mash and place it in a roasting pan in the preheated oven. Allow the fat to melt for 1 hour or more, until mostly liquid. Ladle the melted fat into a 9 by 13-inch baking dish. Discard the crust of unmelted solids.

Allow the baking dish to cool on the counter, then place it in the refrigerator overnight.

Cut the fat into fifteen 2-ounce (about ¼-cup) pieces, wrap the squares in aluminum foil, then store in the refrigerator for up to 1 week or the freezer for up to 3 months.

CHILI QUEENS

Back in the late nineteenth century, chili had a sexy reputation. The idea that spicy foods incite illicit passions was part of the dish's early allure—an allure that was personified by the so-called "Chili Queens" of San Antonio. In the 1880s, the chili stands of San Antonio's Laredito barrio were located on the edge of the red light district. A chili stand called Madame Garza's " . . . was frequented by pimps, gamblers, and courtesans as well as by the best people," one writer observed. "The two worlds had a rare opportunity to study each other over a bowl of chili."

Fascination with the saleswomen who called themselves "Chili Queens" (occasionally spelled "Chile Queens") was one of the main reasons chili con carne became so well known across the country. Accounts of the exotic Chili Queens began to appear in Midwestern newspapers shortly after the railroads connected Texas and Chicago. In the 1880s, San Antonio became a popular tourist destination for rail travelers. The city's Mexican Quarter was considered the most exciting late-night scene in the country.

By the late 1800s, an elaborate sort of outdoor restaurant had evolved. Three ten-foot planks were propped on sawhorses and covered with red and white-checkered oilcloth, explained occasional San Antonio resident William Sydney Porter, better known as O. Henry.

The tables were decorated with vases of paper flowers and lit by laundry lamps. Patrons availed themselves of condiments from red clay dishes that contained oregano and chopped onions, among other things. In O. Henry's day, a bowl of chili with bread and water sold for ten cents.

A Chili Queen

In his famous short story, "The Enchanted Kiss," Henry writes about "delectable chile-con-carne . . . composed of delicate meats minced with aromatic herbs and the poignant chile Colorado—a compound full of singular savor and a fiery zest."

Dr. Marci R. McMahon, an assistant professor of literature at the University of Texas–Pan American, points out that as female entrepreneurs, the Chili Queens of San Antonio challenged standard assumptions that many Americans held in the early 1900s. Their public fame as businesswomen defied the gender roles of that time. And their proud representation of Latino culture and cuisine flew in face of the era's anti-immigrant rhetoric and the "Americanization" programs that attempted to rapidly assimilate Mexican Americans into the mainstream.

TOURISTS AND CHILI QUEENS

"When the northern tourist used to strike the town, the first things the patriotic citizen who was doing the honors would proudly steer him up against would be the Alamo plaza chili stand, with its attendant divinity, the far famed chili queen.

'Now, sir, you've seen the historic Alamo, the old cathedral and the missions and got a whiff of our ozone,' the citizen would remark with righteous pride, 'and tonight you must come and eat a Mexican supper and see the chili queens. The chili queens are one of our most noted attractions—the beautiful, dark eyed senoritas, you know.'

The tourist generally knew. This was in the late eighties, the palmy days of the chili queens, when their fame had spread to the larger northern cities. Some very musical verse about them had appeared in the magazines, and in the newspaper sketches they were idealized as stunning creatures, with the rich, brown skins of the tropics and the languorous grace and bewitching black eyes of Spanish donnas.

They all used the Spanish dialect when they had special customers, despite the fact that other tongues came easier to some of them by nature. There were six reigning queens on the plaza in 1888, and one of them was of German descent and another was born in the island where the sod is highly green and there are no snakes. The other four, however, were senoritas of the genuine Mexican variety.

'Well, let's begin on our chili peppers,' suggests the citizen. 'You say you never ate one before? We had better take a little of everything, then, so you can say you 'did' San Antonio right. Bring us the whole bill of fare, Chiquita.'

'Jesus, andarle! Dos platas de chili con carne, y dos tamales con chili gravy, de enchilades tortillas, y dos tazas de cafe.'

The fiercely burning chili con carne agonizes the tourist and he chokes on the enchilades, but he manages to struggle through the tamales by drinking a great deal of water. . . .When it comes time to go, he insists on paying the bill, despite protests of the citizen, and tenders a $5 bill. Chiquita seems to have trouble in counting out the change and a thought strikes the tourist.

'Say, Chiquita," he says tentatively, 'you needn't mind that if—'

'You mean you want to make me a present?' She tucks the bill in her bosom, and gives the tourist a fond look . . . and squeezes his hand in bidding him goodby.

The glory of the chili queens waned and flickered away with great suddenness, and they themselves drifted away from the high tide of fame and fortune in a like manner."

—*Stevens Point* (WI) Daily Journal,
November 3, 1897

Chili stand in Haymarket Plaza, circa 1904 →

DRIED CHILE PASTE

Before chili powder was patented and sold commercially in the 1890s by William Gebhardt, chili con carne was made with whole dried chiles that had been softened in a hot liquid. A puree made from whole dried chiles gives a pot of chili a silky smooth texture. You can use it instead of chili powder or use a combination of the two. Ancho chiles are the main ingredient in Texas chilis, but the combination of two or more dried chiles makes for a well-rounded flavor.

MAKES 4 CUPS

5 cloves garlic, unpeeled

2 ounces dried ancho chiles (6 to 8, depending on size), seeded and stemmed

11 cups water

1 ounce dried guajillo or New Mexican long red (for a reddish puree) or pasilla chile (for a darker, sharper-tasting puree), seeded and stemmed

1½ teaspoons salt

2 tablespoons tallow or lard (or substitute vegetable oil)

Put the garlic cloves in a large skillet, griddle, or *comal* and toast them over high heat, turning several times to char the peel. Remove them from the heat and allow to cool. Remove the peel.

In a pot, bring 8 cups of the water to a boil. Turn off the heat. Seed and stem the chiles and rinse them to remove any dust from the skin. Place them in the hot water. Place a plate on top of the chiles to submerge them and allow them to soak for 1 hour. Remove the chiles and place them in a blender with the garlic. Add the salt. Add the remaining 3 cups of water and process on high for 5 minutes.

Pour the puree through a strainer into a mixing bowl or large measuring cup, using a spatula or a wooden spoon to push it through. Extract as much puree as possible and discard the skin left in the strainer.

In a skillet or pot over medium-high heat, melt the fat or heat the oil. Reduce the heat to low and add the strained chile puree. Simmer for 5 minutes, stirring with a spoon to prevent sticking. Remove the pot from the heat and allow the puree to cool. Use immediately or reserve the puree for use in other recipes. It will keep in a sealed container in the refrigerator for up to 4 days or the freezer for up to 3 months.

RICHARD BOLT'S "DEVILED BEEF"

This chili is cooked in the old style without searing or browning the meat. The beef and tallow are mixed with water, boiled until the meat is tender, then combined with seasonings. The recipe comes from a cookbook by Richard Bolt titled *Forty Years Behind the Lid*. Richard Bolt worked until the 1970s as a chuck wagon cook for the 6666 Ranch in Guthrie, Texas (known as the Four Sixes). He learned at the knee of a master—his father was an old-time trail drive *cocinero*, as chuck wagon cooks are known in Spanish. His dad called his chili "deviled beef" and cooked it in a cast-iron Dutch oven over the smoldering coals of a campfire.

SERVES 4

4 ounces (½ cup) suet, finely chopped suet, or rendered tallow

2 pounds chopped or ground beef (chili grind if possible)

1 onion, chopped

1 cup Dried Chile Paste (page 73), or ¼ cup Homemade Chili Powder (page 11)

2 teaspoons salt

½ teaspoon ground cumin

½ teaspoon garlic powder

2 tablespoons masa harina, or ¼ cup cracker meal (see sidebar), to thicken (optional)

Saltines, to serve

Chopped raw onion, to serve

Combine the suet and chili meat in a Dutch oven and cover with enough water to bring the level about 1 inch over the meat. Cook, uncovered, over medium heat until the meat is tender, about 1 hour. Add the onion, chile puree, salt, cumin, and garlic powder and cook for 30 minutes, adding water as necessary to maintain a desired consistency.

To make a smoother chili, thicken with masa mixed in an equal amount of hot water or stir in some cracker meal and cook until thickened.

Serve with saltines and chopped raw onions.

CRACKER MEAL

Chili parlors served chili with saltines or oyster crackers so diners could crumble the crackers up to thicken the chili and make the spicy orange grease more palatable. Some chili cooks thickened their chili with cracker meal instead of masa harina or cornmeal.

Cracker meal was once common in grocery stores—it was also used as a coating when frying fish or chicken. But it has become hard to find. You can substitute matzo meal if you can find it, or simply make your own cracker meal by putting saltines in a ziplock bag and crushing them with a rolling pin. Crushing 30 saltine crackers makes about 1 cup of cracker meal.

PENDERGRAST'S GRASS-FED BEEF CHILI

The rangy old longhorns that provided the meat for the earliest versions of chili con carne "bore little resemblance to the beef cattle of today. To make a proper chili, steer clear of the top grades and go to the bottom of the livestock quotations where you will find listed 'bologna bulls' and 'chili bulls'," wrote Charles Pendergrast in his history of "The National Dish of Texas." According to Pendergrast, the cheaper cuts are actually superior when it comes to chili—the expensive, highly marbled meat just turns to mush.

Pendergrast's approach to chili is perfect for those who favor grass-fed beef. Most people buy grass-fed beef to avoid the hormones and antibiotics in conventional beef—not because they want less marbling. Ask your grass-fed beef source to sell you some suet along with the meat, and you will have the perfect ingredients for Pendergrast's version of old-fashioned chili.

SERVES 5

2½ pounds grass-fed beef chuck

1 pound (about 2 cups) suet or rendered tallow from grass-fed beef

2 cups Dried Chile Paste (page 73), or ½ cup Homemade Chili Powder (page 11)

¼ cup paprika

3 tablespoons ground cumin

4 cups water

¼ cup garlic powder

1 tablespoon salt

Cracker meal (optional)

In a Dutch oven over medium-high heat, combine the meat and fat and cook until the meat turns a grayish color and the fat melts, about 30 minutes. Add the chile puree, paprika, and cumin. Stir to combine. Add the water and bring to a boil. Reduce to a simmer and cook for 3 hours. Add the garlic powder and salt.

You can serve each bowl of chili with some of the orange grease from the top of the pot, add some cracker meal (see page 74) to thicken it, or skim the grease off and reserve to make Pendergast's Old-Fashioned Chili Gravy (see box below and variation at right).

"When chili is properly made, a thick layer of red chili oil will rise to the top. Whatever you do, don't throw this grease away—it contains the flavor and essence of the chili," according to Charles Pendergrast.

Pendergrast suggests you combine the oil with flour, cook it a little and either return it to the chili, or thin it with stock—this is the origin of that Tex-Mex sauce, "chili gravy."

VARIATION

Old-Fashioned Chili Gravy Skim ⅓ cup chili oil from the top of a pot of chili and place in a skillet over medium-high heat. Whisk in ⅓ cup flour and cook for 2 minutes, or until the flour is no longer raw. Add 4 cups water or beef stock to the skillet a little at a time and whisk until all of the flour mixture is dissolved. Continue stirring until the gravy thickens, adding more stock as necessary to reach a desired consistency. Use the chili gravy as an enchilada sauce or combine it with an equal amount of chili con carne to make a "chili mix" that can be used as an enchilada sauce or as a topping on a chili dog, chili burger, or chili fries.

A cowboy dishes chili on a ranch near Marfa, 1939. (Photo by Russell Lee)

LONGHORNS, CHILI QUEENS, AND THE CRADLE OF TEXAS CHILI

CHILI QUEEN CHILI

San Antonio chili con carnes were often cooked in earthen *cazuelas* over smoldering coals. This 1930s recipe from a San Antonio restaurant is based on an original Chili Queen recipe. The pork added some extra fat. Much like a French *daube*, the earliest chili con carnes called for the raw meat to be combined with the liquids without browning or searing.

SERVES 6

5½ cups water

1 pound pork shoulder, cut in ½-inch dice

2 pounds beef chuck, cut in ½-inch dice

4 ounces (½ cup) rendered tallow

2 tablespoons salt

2 tablespoons cumin seeds, toasted and freshly ground

1 tablespoon finely ground black pepper

6 cloves garlic, minced

2 serrano chiles, finely chopped

1 teaspoon sugar

2 cups Dried Chile Paste (page 73)

Flour, as needed

Heat the water in a soup pot over high heat. Add the pork, beef, tallow, salt, cumin, black pepper, garlic, serrano chiles, and sugar and bring to a boil. Reduce the heat and simmer for 35 minutes. Add the chili puree and simmer 30 minutes more.

Skim the orange fat off the top of the chili and combine in a skillet over medium heat with an equal amount of flour and stir until the flour is cooked, about 2 minutes. Add the chili roux back to the cooked chili a spoonful at a time, stirring after each addition, and cook until thickened, 2 to 3 minutes. Serve in a bowl or as a topping for tamales or enchiladas.

FIDEO CON CARNE

This was a favorite dish of Lydia Mendoza, the Queen of Tejano music, who started her career serenading the crowds that gathered on the plaza while the Chili Queens were cooking.

Fideo is the Spanish word for pasta or macaroni. Toasting pasta or rice before cooking is a technique introduced by the Arabs to Spain. This technique is used in Mexican "sopa seca," or dry soup—it's something like a pilaf (from the Turkish word *pilav*).

Fideo con carne became a favorite campfire meal among South Texas cowboys. It is made with ground beef, chili powder, tomato, onions, and the vermicelli fragments called fideo. If you can't find fideo in a box at the grocery store, just break ⅓ pound of regular vermicelli into 2-inch pieces with your hands, or use *conchitas*, the small-size pasta shells.

SERVES 4

3 tablespoons tallow
(or substitute vegetable oil)

1 pound ground beef

½ onion, chopped

2 cloves garlic, minced

2 jalapeños, chopped

1 (15-ounce) can tomato sauce

5 to 7 ounces fideo

½ cup water, plus more
if needed

1 tablespoon chili powder,
homemade (page 11)
or store-bought

1 teaspoon dried
Mexican oregano

Heat 2 tablespoons of the tallow in a sauté pan over medium-high heat. Brown the meat for 5 to 7 minutes until nicely colored and add the onion, garlic, and chiles. Continue cooking until the onion is soft, another 5 to 7 minutes. Add the tomato sauce and stir well. Reduce to a simmer.

Heat the remaining 1 tablespoon of tallow in a skillet over medium-high heat. Add the pasta to the skillet and stir until nicely browned, about 3 minutes. Add the browned pasta to the meat mixture. Add ½ cup water and the chili powder and oregano and stir well to combine. Cover and simmer, stirring often, until the pasta is soft, 5 to 10 minutes. Add more water if the mixture becomes too dry. Serve immediately.

FRIJOLES REFRITOS

The mashed potatoes of Tex-Mex, refried beans are the universal side dish. While the secret of tasty mashed potatoes is lots of butter, the secret of tasty refried beans is lots of lard. Pinto beans are traditional, but black beans are very tasty and white beans are always a pleasant surprise. (See the note on cooking beans on page 121.)

Serve with huevos rancheros (page 42) or as a side with any chili—roll up the refried beans, some chili, and shredded cheese in warm flour tortillas to make tacos.

MAKES 6 SIDE SERVINGS

¼ cup lard or bacon drippings (or substitute vegetable oil)

3 cups cooked beans (see page 121), drained

½ teaspoon salt, or more to taste

½ cup reserved bean broth or water

⅛ teaspoon finely ground black pepper

Melt the lard in a large skillet over medium-high heat and heat for 1 minute. Add the beans and mash them for 2 minutes with a fork or potato masher. Stir in salt and adjust to taste. Add the bean broth and the black pepper and continue mashing until the beans reach the desired consistency, then serve. Tex-Mex beans are generally chunky rather than soupy. The beans will thicken more as they cool.

CHAPTER 5
COMIDA TEX-MEX

Chili is the mother sauce of Tex-Mex. It is to old-fashioned Tex-Mex what red sauce is to Italian-American cooking. You make a large pot of it, and then you use it to make other dishes. Texans don't put beans in the chili for the same reason that Italian-Americans don't dump spaghetti into the red sauce.

Early Tex-Mex restaurant menus were modeled after the Original Mexican Restaurant, which was opened in San Antonio in 1899 by a Chicagoan named Otis Farnsworth. In the late 1890s, while visiting the chili stands of San Antonio, Farnsworth was shocked that Anglos in fancy clothes were lining up to eat at such makeshift eateries in the barrio. He came up with the idea of building an elegant Mexican restaurant for Anglos in the commercial district and staffing it with Latinos.

Farnsworth hired a famous German muralist to paint scenes of Mexican peasants on the walls. In this upscale Mexican restaurant, gentlemen were required to wear jackets.

The Original became the most successful Mexican restaurant in the nation. Chili con carne featured prominently on the menu, where it was combined with spaghetti, scrambled eggs, tamales, and other items.

At the time, chili con carne, and all of the foods prepared and sold by the Spanish-speaking citizens of Texas were called Mexican food. The industry that began with Gebhardt's chili powder expanded with the success of competitors such as Walker's Austex in Austin; makers of Mexene "Red Devil" chili powder, and Walker's Austex "Red Hot" Chile con Carne. Because it was marketed to Americans as authentic Mexican food, the elite of Mexico City have a special contempt for Tex-Mex chili con carne, which was defined in the *Diccionario de Mejicanismos* as a "detestable comida que con el falso titulo de mejicana"—that is, "a detestable food falsely labeled Mexican."

As Americans learned more about the cuisine of interior Mexico—the complex moles, elegant stuffed squash blossoms, and exotic huitlacoche dishes—Tex-Mex cooking started to fall out of fashion. (Although "authentic Mexican" restaurants in Texas ended up carrying on Tex-Mex traditions because their customers still demanded chips and salsa, nachos, and frozen margaritas.)

Recently, Tex-Mex has begun to make a comeback. Restaurants that insisted for years that they served authentic Mexican food have lately changed their minds and decided to fly the Tex-Mex banner. In 2010, I joined chef Bryan Caswell and restaurateur Bill Floyd in opening El Real Tex-Mex Café in Houston,

a restaurant that celebrates "vintage Tex-Mex" with a menu of old-fashioned dishes from all over the state. And chili con carne is at the heart of our cooking.

At El Real, our chili is made with freshly ground chili powder and ½-inch beef chuck pieces sautéed in bacon drippings. It's served by itself in a bowl with a fried egg on top and in Frito Pie. Our "chili mix" is half chili and half chili gravy, and it's used as an enchilada sauce and as a topping for combination plates. "Chili mix" is also served on the Tampiqueño plate, a rib-eye steak topped with two cheese enchiladas and chili.

Among an older generation of food snobs, Tex-Mex will always be seen as inferior to "real Mexican food." But to the new generation of food lovers, Tex-Mex has come to be seen as an honest regional American cuisine with deep historical roots—and a fascinating part of Americana.

> "Tex-Mex food might be described as native foreign food, contradictory though that term may seem. It is native, for it does not exist elsewhere; it was born on this soil. But it is foreign in that its inspiration came from an alien cuisine; that it has never merged into the mainstream of American cooking and remains alive almost solely in the region where it originated . . . "
>
> —Waverly Root & Richard de Rochemont, *Eating in America*

EL REAL'S CHILI CON CARNE

This is the way we make chili at El Real Tex-Mex Cafe in Houston. Be sure and use the Homemade Chili Powder (page 11) for a full-flavored chili. Don't skip the step of dry toasting the cumin seeds; it really improves the flavor.

SERVES 6

2 tablespoons cumin seeds

8 ounces bacon, chopped

3 pounds beef chuck, cut into ¼-inch cubes

2 onions, chopped

¼ cup Homemade Chili Powder (page 11)

2 teaspoons sweet paprika

1 teaspoon dried Mexican oregano

1 teaspoon freshly ground black pepper

½ teaspoon dried thyme

½ teaspoon salt

4 large cloves garlic, minced

1¾ cups beef broth

1 (28-ounce) can pureed tomatoes

2 dried ancho chiles, stemmed and seeded

Toast the cumin seeds in a large skillet over medium-high heat until fragrant, about 1 to 2 minutes. Using a smaller frying pan or a metal or wooden tool with a flat surface, crush the seeds coarsely. Set aside.

Cook the bacon in the skillet over medium-high heat until crisp. Remove the bacon and reserve. Over high heat, brown the beef in the bacon drippings left in the skillet and set the meat aside. Over medium heat, sauté the onions in the remaining drippings until lightly browned, 8 to 10 minutes.

Add the toasted cumin, chili powder, paprika, oregano, black pepper, thyme, salt, and garlic to the cooked onions and sauté for 1 minute. Crumble in the bacon, add the beef broth, 1 cup of water, the tomatoes, ancho chiles, and the beef.

Bring to a boil, reduce the heat, cover partially, and simmer until the meat is very tender, about 2 hours, adding water as needed to maintain the desired consistency.

Alternatively, transfer to a slow-cooker set on low and cook for at least 6 hours and up to 8 hours, until the meat is very tender.

Remove the anchos, puree in a blender, and return to the pot. Serve in a bowl with chopped onions and shredded cheese, with saltines, over tamales, rice or potatoes, in a Frito Pie or combined with beans.

RESTAURANT CHILI GRAVY

The first chili gravies were made with grease skimmed off the top of the chili pot (see page 67). Restaurant chili gravy tastes like a cross between Anglo brown gravy and Mexican red chile sauce.

MAKES 2 CUPS

¼ cup lard (or substitute vegetable oil)

¼ cup flour

½ teaspoon finely ground black pepper

1 teaspoon salt

1½ teaspoons garlic powder

2 teaspoons ground cumin

½ teaspoon dried Mexican oregano

2 tablespoons Homemade Chili Powder (page 11)

2 cups chicken broth or water

Heat the lard in a skillet over medium-high heat. Stir in the flour and continue stirring until it makes a very light brown roux, 3 to 4 minutes. Add the black pepper, salt, garlic powder, cumin, oregano, and chili powder and continue to cook for 1 minute, constantly stirring and blending the ingredients. Add the chicken broth, mixing and stirring until the sauce thickens. Turn the heat to low and let simmer for 15 minutes. Add water to adjust the thickness. Use immediately as an enchilada topping or mix half and half with El Real's Chili Con Carne (page 87) to make a sauce for chili dogs, chili burgers, or chili fries.

A. J. FOYT'S SUPERTEX-MEX CHORIZO CHILI

A. J. Foyt grew up in Houston, and his nickname on the professional racing circuit was "SuperTex." Foyt still holds the record for automobile racing wins; he is also the only man to win four Indianapolis 500 races. His chili recipe includes authentic Houston ingredients, like a pound of chorizo and a can of Mexican beer.

SERVES 8

3 tablespoons olive oil

3 pounds beef chuck roast, cubed

1 pound fresh chorizo, homemade (page 33) or store-bought

2 large onions, diced

5 cloves garlic, minced

3 fresh jalapeño chiles, chopped

½ teaspoon cayenne pepper

3 tablespoons chili powder, homemade (page 11) or store-bought

3 (15-ounce) cans tomato sauce

1 teaspoon salt

1 (12-ounce) can Mexican beer

2 cups water, plus more as needed

Heat the oil in a Dutch oven over medium-high heat. Add the beef in batches and cook 5 to 7 minutes or until browned, transferring the browned meat to a plate with a slotted spoon. When the beef is browned, add the chorizo and cook 5 to 7 minutes or until no pink remains, scraping with a spatula to turn. When the chorizo is cooked, add the onions, garlic, and jalapeños and stir while adding the cayenne and chili powder. Add the tomato sauce, salt, beer, and water. Return the beef to the pot. Cover and cook over low heat for 30 minutes, stirring often. Uncover and simmer for 2 hours, adding water as necessary to maintain the desired consistency.

Alternatively, transfer the beef and sauce mixture to a slow-cooker set on low and cook for at least 6 hours and up to 8 hours, or until the meat is tender and the flavors are well blended.

Serve with bottles of Mexican beer dressed with salt and lime quarters.

OLD-FASHIONED TEX-MEX ENCHILADAS

This is the best-selling item at El Real, and some say the best cheese enchiladas in the state of Texas. Try them with a fried egg on top!

SERVES 12 (2 ENCHILADAS PER PERSON)

½ cup lard (or substitute vegetable oil)

24 store-bought yellow corn tortillas

1 pound Velveeta, shredded or chopped

2 large onions, chopped

2 cups El Real's Chili con Carne (page 87)

2 cups Restaurant Chili Gravy (page 88)

1 pound cheddar cheese, shredded

Preheat the oven to 400°F. Set 2 or 3 large Pyrex baking pans next to the stove.

Heat the lard in a small skillet over medium heat until it sizzles. Using tongs, dip each tortilla in the hot lard for 30 seconds, or until soft and pliable. Don't let the oil get too hot. Place each tortilla in a baking pan and put ¼ cup of Velveeta cheese and a tablespoon of onion across the middle. Roll up the tortilla and place it seam side down. Continue rolling tortillas and packing them close together in the Pyrex pans.

Mix the chile con carne and chili gravy together to make an enchilada sauce and divide it among the pans, spreading on top of the enchiladas. Sprinkle generously with shredded cheddar. Bake for about 10 minutes, until the cheese on top begins to bubble. Remove from the oven, top with remaining chopped onion and serve immediately.

VARIATIONS

Enchilada Plates Prepare the enchiladas on individual ovenproof plates instead of in baking pans. Place under the broiler to melt the cheese, then top with chopped onions and a fried egg. Serve with rice and beans.

FRITO PIE

New Mexicans say Teresa Hernandez invented the Frito pie in the 1960s at the Santa Fe Woolworth's (now the Five & Dime General Store), ladling her mom's homemade red chile with pork directly into the corn chip bags with no garnishes. Texans, meanwhile, claim that the dish was invented in San Antonio by Daisy Dean Doolin, the mother of Fritos inventor Charles Elmer Doolin, in the 1930s.

Actually, both origin stories are myths according to the 2011 book *Fritos Pie: Stories, Recipes, and More*, by Charles Doolin's daughter Kaleta Doolin. Daisy Dean gets credit for the company's 1937 "Cooking with Fritos" campaign, which first championed the corn chip's culinary versatility in the test kitchens for the Frito consumer service department. The popularity of Frito pie soared in 1962, when this recipe appeared on millions of bags of chips: "Heat can of chili, pour into bag of Fritos, and sprinkle with shredded cheese and chopped onions." Here's a more elaborate recipe and a few famous variations.

SERVES 4

4 cups Fritos corn chips

2½ cups El Real's
Chili con Carne (page 87)
or another meat chili

½ cup finely chopped onions

2 cups shredded
cheddar cheese

¼ cup jalapeño slices
(optional)

Preheat the oven to 350°F.

Put the corn chips in the bottom of a small baking pan and spread the chili evenly over the top. Sprinkle with onions, shredded cheddar, and jalapeños. Bake for 5 minutes, or until cheese is melted. Use a spatula to transfer the servings to plates or bowls.

VARIATIONS

New Mexican Frito Pie Substitute Chile Colorado con Puerco (see page 35) for the meat chili and top each serving with a dollop of sour cream and some chopped green onions.

Original Frito Pie Open a 1¾-ounce bag of Fritos corn chips. Into the bag, pour ½ cup chili, ¼ cup shredded cheddar, 1 tablespoon chopped onion, and a couple of jalapeño slices. Eat it out of the bag.

Taco-Style Frito Pie Top each serving with ½ cup shredded iceberg lettuce and a ¼ cup chopped tomatoes.

Shaggy Dog Frito Pie Dump a 1¾-ounce bag of Fritos over a hot dog on a bun, pour ½ cup of chili over the chips and hot dog, sprinkle 1 tablespoon of chopped onions and shredded cheese on top.

CHILI COOK-OFFS

When Dallas newspaper columnist Frank X. Tolbert wrote an article titled "That Bowl of Fire Called Chili" for the *Saturday Evening Post* in 1962, it generated thousands of letters. Tolbert expanded his thoughts into a book titled *A Bowl of Red*, which was published in 1966.

In 1967, to promote his book, Tolbert organized a famous chili cook-off in Terlingua, Texas. The event was sponsored by Californian Carroll Shelby, the Texas-born race car driver who was attempting to develop real estate in the Big Bend area.

Dave Chasen of Chasen's in Beverly Hills, a restaurant that was once famous for its chili, dropped out of the contest and was replaced by H. Allen Smith, a Midwesterner living in New York who wrote an article in *Holiday* magazine titled, "Nobody Knows More about Chili Than I Do." Texas was represented by another newspaper man, Homer "Wick" Fowler. The famous Terlingua chili contest launched the modern cook-off era. It was declared a draw—mainly because the participants were already banking on a sequel.

The first Texas chili cook-off was actually held 15 years earlier at the 1952 Texas State Fair in Dallas by another newspaper man, Joe E. Cooper, to publicize his book, *With or Without Beans: An Informal Biography of Chili*. The winner of that first contest was Mrs. F. G. Ventura, of Dallas. Her recipe was nearly identical to the one on the back of the Gebhardt chili powder bottle.

Created by journalists, the chili cook-offs made for colorful newspaper and magazine copy. The contestants competed on "battlefields." Allegations of cheating, prejudiced judges, and opposing factions were chronicled in tongue-in-cheek books such as *The Great Chili Confrontation*. Arguments over whether or not to add beans to chili were delivered in rants and screeds.

Bickering over television rights divided the chili cook-off crowd into two camps. Frank X. Tolbert headed the Chili Appreciation Society International (CASI) faction. Carroll Shelby broke ties to form the International Chili Society (ICS). Each group still sponsors its own series of chili cook-offs.

The chili cook-offs succeeded in making Americans aware of the original Texas version of chili con carne. But you couldn't really say that awareness caused people all over the country to change their preferences in chili. Instead, the takeaway seemed to be that Texans have a bizarre and irrational aversion to putting beans in their chili.

Terlingua Cook-Off poster by Adam Guy Hays →

WICK FOWLER'S ORIGINAL FOUR ALARM CHILI

The recipe that won Wick Fowler so many cook-offs was a whole lot hotter than the Wick Fowler 2-Alarm Chili Mix he later sold through grocery stores. The original included Tabasco pepper sauce, chili powder, cayenne pepper, whole chile pequíns, and whole dried japones chiles. (Fowler counseled that chile eaters should decide for themselves if they wanted to mash the whole peppers for additional heat.) If your mouth feels like it's on fire after eating this, drink a glass of buttermilk—that's the remedy recommended by chili cook-off judges.

Fowler recommended hand-chopped beef chuck, cleaned of gristle and cut into pieces the size of the last joint of your little finger.

SERVES 6 TO 8

3 pounds finely chopped beef chuck or ground beef, chili grind preferred

1½ cups canned tomato sauce

1 teaspoon Tabasco sauce

3 heaping tablespoons chili powder, homemade (page 11) or store-bought

1 teaspoon dried Mexican oregano

1 teaspoon ground cumin

2 onions, chopped

6 cloves garlic, chopped

1 teaspoon salt

1 teaspoon cayenne pepper

1 tablespoon sweet paprika

3 tablespoons flour, for thickening

6 to 8 chile pequíns

12 or more whole dried japones chiles

Cook the meat over medium-high heat in a Dutch oven until browned, 5 to 7 minutes. Add the tomato sauce and enough water to cover the meat by ½ inch, and mix well. Stir in the Tabasco, chili powder, oregano, cumin, onions, garlic, salt, cayenne, and paprika. Let simmer for 1 hour.

Skim the grease off the top of the pot and discard. Mix the flour with an equal amount of water to make a slurry without lumps. Add the slurry to the pot, increase the heat, and blend thoroughly until it thickens. Adjust the seasonings. Put the chile pequíns and japones chiles in the pot, but do not break them open. For the best flavor, Fowler recommends refrigerating the chili overnight; reheat and serve the next day.

To serve, ladle a serving of chili in a bowl and float a japones chile on the top as a garnish. Pass a bowl of chopped onions and a bowl of chile pequíns around the table. Serve with pinto beans on the side.

BOB PLAGER'S $25,000 CHILI

This chili won veteran cook-off competitor Bob Plager $25,000 at the 2012 International Chili Society's World's Championship Chili Cookoff in Charleston, West Virginia. Plager has been competing in chili cook-offs since the 1980s. He met his wife, Kathy, at a chili cook-off where she was also a competitor. Bob and Kathy Plager often compete as a husband-and-wife team. Prunes are the secret ingredient in this award-winning recipe; they bring a hint of sweetness to the flavor and an appealing gloss to the bowl. Adding spices in several stages creates a greater depth of flavor.

SERVES 4

1 tablespoon solid vegetable shortening, such as Crisco

2¼ pounds beef tri-tip roast, trimmed of fat and gristle and cut into small cubes

1½ cups beef broth

1½ cups chicken broth

1 (8-ounce) can tomato sauce

2 pitted prunes

FIRST SPICES

1 tablespoon paprika

1 teaspoon onion powder

1 teaspoon garlic powder

2 teaspoons beef bouillon granules

1 teaspoon chicken bouillon granules

½ teaspoon salt

½ tablespoon ground New Mexican long red chile

½ tablespoon New Mexican light chili powder

In a Dutch oven over high heat, melt the shortening. Add the meat and brown until no visible pink remains, stirring and scraping as necessary. Drain and discard the grease, leaving the meat in the pot. Add the beef broth, chicken broth, tomato sauce, and prunes. Add all the spices under the heading First Spices. Bring to a boil, then lower the heat, cover the pot, and simmer for approximately 2 hours, stirring occasionally.

Remove the prunes (they might explode otherwise) and add water as necessary to maintain desired consistency.

About 30 minutes before serving, add all the spices under the heading Second Spices. Stir to mix well and continue to simmer for 15 minutes. Add the seasonings under the heading Third Spices. Stir to mix well and continue cooking over low heat for 15 minutes. Just before serving, correct the seasonings with additional salt and Tabasco sauce, if necessary.

SECOND SPICES

1 tablespoon ground cumin

½ teaspoon garlic powder

½ teaspoon onion powder

½ teaspoon freshly ground
black pepper

½ teaspoon salt

1½ teaspoons Gebhardt
brand chili powder

1½ teaspoons Texas-style
chili powder

1½ teaspoons ground
New Mexican long red chile

1½ teaspoons New Mexican
light chili powder

THIRD SPICES

2 teaspoons Texas-style
chili powder

1 teaspoon ground cumin

Salt

Tabasco sauce

COOK-OFF RULES

NO FILLERS IN CHILI: Beans, macaroni, rice, hominy, or other similar ingredients are not permitted.
—Official CASI Rules & Guidelines

The prohibition of beans is one of the only things CASI and ICS agreed on. When chili cook-offs became popular in the reasonable realm of the Midwest, the rules were simply changed to allow for local tastes. At the 2014 Lenexa Chili Challenge in Lenexa, Kansas, there were two categories, which were defined as follows:

CASI CHILI is described as any kind of meat or combination of meats cooked with chili peppers, various other spices, and other ingredients, with the exception of items such as beans or spaghetti, which are strictly forbidden.

HOME STYLE CHILI is described as any kind of meat, meat substitution or no meat (vegetarian) cooked with various spices and other ingredients, which may include any variety of beans, spaghetti, or other fillers. Home Style may also include "non-red" chili.

SENATOR KAY BAILEY HUTCHINSON'S CONGRESSIONAL COOK-OFF CHAMPIONSHIP CHILI

Evidently, the CASI rules were not in effect at the annual Congressional Chili Cook-off the year that Texas Senator Kay Bailey Hutchinson won. Here is her account:

"Did I discover the key to world peace? Judging from the attention I received, one might have thought so. But no, it was a chili contest that garnered all that attention—and I won! I recaptured for Texas the coveted Congressional Club Chili Cook-Off championship.

"Of course, every triumph brings controversy in its wake. . . . As you might guess, most of the criticism aimed at the chili which I submitted focused on our use of one highly controversial ingredient. If you're a native Texan, you would immediately say . . . of course . . . beans!

"I have long been aware of the vast chasm stretching across Texas that separates the pro-beans-in-chili advocates from the anti-beans-in-chili purists. It is closely akin to the long-standing rivalry between Longhorns and Aggie fans. . . .But there were other points of criticism aimed at our chili recipe, as well. Several commentators objected to the use of kidney rather than pinto beans. This was actually a decision based on necessity, bean selection here in Washington being limited.

"Houston columnist Leon Hale, whom I otherwise have always admired, took issue with the inclusion of green peppers. I admit this is borderline. But surely it's an exaggeration to assert, as he did, that such ingredients add up to a 'recipe for disaster.'

"Regardless of such debate, I am proud to have represented my state so successfully and to have returned the trophy to its rightful place: in the office of a United States Senator from Texas. It has been won by members of Congress from other states for five years—now that is a scandal!!"

—Senator Kay Bailey Hutchinson

SERVES 5

2 yellow onions, diced

2 green bell peppers, diced

1 tablespoon olive oil

Salt and freshly ground
black pepper

Garlic powder

2½ pounds ground sirloin

3 to 4 tablespoons mole sauce

2 (8-ounce) cans tomato sauce

½ cup chili powder

1 (16-ounce) can kidney beans

Sauté half the onion and peppers in 1½ teaspoons of the olive oil over medium-high heat. Add salt, pepper, and garlic to taste. Brown the meat separately over medium-high heat, leaving it in chunks. Drain the fat. Add the onion/pepper mixture to the meat. Add 3 tablespoons of the mole to the mixture. Transfer to a large pot. Add the tomato sauce, 2 to 3 cans water, and 3 tablespoons of the chili powder. Bring to a boil. Add the remaining 1 tablespoon mole, if desired. Simmer for 1 hour. Season and stir occasionally.

Sauté the remaining onions and peppers in the remaining olive oil as above. Add to the pot, along with drained beans. Add the remaining 1 tablespoon chili powder or add to taste. Continue simmering for about 15 minutes until everything is heated through, then serve.

CHILI ROAD TRIP

CHAPTER 6
ROUTE 66 AND OTHER KICKS

Chili con carne was a sensation at the Chicago World's Fair of 1893. In the days before movies or television, attending a world's fair was the height of entertainment. Hundreds of thousands of attendees from all over the country swarmed the fairgrounds for the 1893 Chicago World's Fair. The fair put chili con carne in the national spotlight with a typical San Antonio chili stand recreated on the fairgrounds that sold chili con carne along with tamales and other creations of the Chili Queens, who were already famous in that part of the country.

O. T. Hodge started selling chili at the 1904 Saint Louis World's Fair. At the conclusion of the fair, Hodge went on to open several chili parlors in Saint Louis. The O. T. Hodge Chile Parlor and Lunch Room chain in Saint Louis offered chili with tamales, chili mac, and a peculiar specialty called a "slinger."

Breakfast "slingers" are the specialty of the vintage Eat-Rite Diner.

I ate my first "slinger" at the Eat-Rite Diner in Saint Louis, where it is served as a breakfast dish. First comes a pile of hash browns and your choice of bacon or sausage (I went for two sausage patties), topped with two eggs (I asked for fried), a large ladle of chili, shredded cheddar cheese, and raw onions. It was a gloriously sloppy mess of a breakfast. I mopped up the chili and yolk with the two slices of toasted white bread that came on the side.

When I asked for the chili recipe, the waitress went back to the freezer and got a two-pound plastic "chub" of frozen chili from Edmonds Chile Co. (which, incidentally, still uses O. T. Hodge's original recipe). The ingredient list on the package revealed the secret of the old-fashioned chili flavor—suet was the number two ingredient after beef.

Eat-Rite Diner is a favorite stopover of travelers on Historic Route 66. The vintage, hundred year-old building looks like the sort of place J. Wellington Wimpy frequented in the Popeye cartoons. The menu is printed on a wrap-around white panel attached to the wall above the grill and cash register.

At other Saint Louis diners, you can get a "slinger" with a hamburger patty, a slice of ham, or a steak instead of breakfast sausages. Variations include extra onions and chili; a mix of chili and white gravy; and hash browns, chili, and cheese without the burger patty. The Saint Louis slinger is traditionally enjoyed in the wee hours of the morning after a few too many cocktails.

As a Texan, I expected to find the oldest chili parlors in America in San Antonio or somewhere in South Texas. But, in fact, some of America's oldest surviving chili joints are in the Midwest.

Fifty miles north of Saint Louis on Historic Route 66, I had the habanero chili at Taylor's Mexican Chili Parlor in Carlinville, Illinois. The chili had a pleasant burn and a large grease slick on top. The grease isn't suet or lard; young, bearded, restaurant owner and head cook Bobby Whitlock told me, it's "oleo oil," a term I'd never heard before, and it's supposed to be soaked up with the crackers that come on the side. The accompanying bowl of creamy butter beans were outstanding. The tamales tasted a little odd; instead of the usual pork filling these were stuffed with Taylor's Mexican chili.

When the parlor opened in 1904, it was attached to the Taylor Mexican Chili factory a few blocks away. The restaurant moved to the current location, next door to the Anchor Inn bar on the town square, in 1998.

The founder of Taylor's Mexican Chili, Charles Taylor, a native of Carlinville, worked in the Mexican National Exhibition at the 1904 Saint Louis World's Fair, where he encountered Mexican food for the first time. No doubt he sampled some of O. T. Hodge's chili while he was there.

The chili canning factory he founded is still in operation at the original location on West Street—in fact, it supplies the chili served at the restaurant. The factory also made the tamales I was eating.

So where did the habanero chili come from?

"I added some extra spices to chili from the factory to make the habanero chili," Whitlock told me. I looked puzzled. "No, I don't actually open cans—I buy the chili in bulk."

But he did have some cans behind the cash register. I bought one when I paid my bill. Taylor's Mexican Chili actually comes in two cans, a small can of beans attached of a larger can of chili. You can eat your chili with or without the beans—the two packages also assure that the beans don't get soggy.

SPRINGFIELD CHILLI

Dew Chilli Parlor: A classic Springfield restaurant recently reopened with new owners. Dew Chilli Parlor's "tavern-style" chili made from quality beef and red kidney beans inspired a host of other chili makers.

Ray's Chilli: Ray DeFrates started producing Ray's Chilli with his brother's recipe. It's still one of the most popular canned chilis in Illinois.

Chilli Man: After working for his Uncle Ray, Joe DeFrates developed his own recipe for canned chili and seasoning mixes. Joe won the World's Championship Chili Cookoff in 1975.

Booker's Tavern Chili: Cigar-chomping former coal miner, Joe Booker created a chili recipe in the 1940s that is the inspiration for Booker's Tavern Chilli seasoning mix.

CHILLI WITH TWO L'S

Fifty miles north of Carlinville on Route 66, in Springfield, Illinois, I stopped by the newly revived Dew Chilli Parlor, which carries on the curious Illinois tradition of spelling chili with two "L"s. The original Dew Chilli Parlor was opened by Fred Crowder in 1909. It was Crowder's battle with a sign painter that resulted in the "chilli" spelling. But it was the restaurant's second owner, Joe Bockelmann, who bought the place after the stock market crash of 1929 and made Dew Chilli Parlor famous.

Bockelmann was still running the place in 1974, when chili earned an honored place in Illinois cuisine. The state legislature established "chilli" as the official Illinois spelling. Governor Daniel Walker issued a special proclamation honoring Joe Bockelmann, and declaring "Two-Ls-in-Chilli Day." A year later, Bockelmann passed away, leaving Dew Chilli to Rita Maurer Patton, a loyal employee of 33 years. In 1995, Rita closed the place.

In 2013, longtime customer Mark Roberts purchased the 1216 S. 5th Street building, which had also been Bockelmann's home, along with the original Dew Chilli recipe from Rita Maurer's family. In 2014, he and his wife reopened the historic Dew Chilli No. 2 with a slightly revised menu. To the Double Header, a favorite on the original menu which combined a tamale and a bowl of chili, the Roberts added The Torpedo (two tamales topped with chilli, cheese, sour cream, corn chips, and sport peppers), The Triple Threat (cheese, onions, and sour cream over a bowl of Dew Chilli), and The Dew-Rrrrrito Pie (a bowl of corn chips smothered with Dew Chilli and topped with cheese, sour cream, and onions).

It's only fitting that Route 66 should be nicknamed "The Will Rogers Highway," since Rogers was a lifelong fan of chili, a dish he called "a bowl of blessedness." In the 1920s, when Rogers had a syndicated newspaper column, he liked to travel around the country hanging out in chili parlors wherever he went. He said he judged a town by the quality of its chili, and he created his own box score system to keep track.

During the 1930s, chili made an inexpensive and nourishing meal for millions of Americans. A bowl of chili was among the cheapest options on the menu at a railroad car diner. At Texas and Oklahoma chili joints, Michigan coney stands, and Ohio chili parlors, you could get a meal for even less than you'd pay at a diner. A newspaper man at the time opined that chili saved more lives during the Great Depression than the Red Cross.

As it crosses the West, Route 66 goes through a lot of Oklahoma and good bit of Texas. Sadly, the chili joints Will Rogers visited in this area in the 1920s and 1930s are gone—but they will live forever in legend. Before it ends at the Santa Monica Pier, Route 66 goes through the Lincoln Heights neighborhood of Los Angeles, once the home Ptomaine Tommy's—the chili joint where the chili burger was invented in the 1920s.

Thomas M. "Ptomaine Tommy" DeForest founded the restaurant around 1913—it went out of business in 1958. My father, who worked for the restaurant division of General Foods, moved our family to Anaheim in 1964, just six years after Tommy's closed. During my time at Sunkist Elementary School, I remember my father coming home from work excited about something he called a "chili size."

He had mom make a pot of chili, and he grilled some hamburgers (page 117). For me, my brothers, and my mom, he place cooked hamburger patties on bottom buns in a bowl, then topped them with chili, some shredded cheese, and a sprinkling of chopped raw onions. The burger sat in a soup bowl with the top bun set to the side—we ate it with a knife and fork. It was the most exotic burger I had ever eaten— which wasn't saying much. The Big Boy Drive-in was my burger benchmark at the time.

My father, who was on a carbohydrate-free diet, made his "chili size" in a bowl without the bun. For most of my childhood, Dad would make himself a chili size whenever my mom made chili. The "size" terminology originated at Ptomaine Tommy's where the shouted order to the line cook, "a size with extra violets," meant a chili burger with extra raw chopped onions.

Speculation about the origin of the term *size* center on the fact that there were two ladles at Tommy's, a large and a small representing two sizes of chili—the large was a full bowl and the small was "hamburger size." Whatever the real story may be, the terms *size* and *chili size* referring to chili burgers became common parlance all over Los Angeles. The term is still understood today. And Southern Californians insist there is no chili burger like an L.A. chili burger.

Route 66 was the highway where Americans invented the road trip and fast food. Red's Giant Hamburg, America's first drive-through restaurant, opened on Route 66 in Springfield, Missouri; the first McDonald's opened just off Route 66 in San Bernadino, California. As American's fondness for fast food grew, chili joints began to fade away—except for a few old joints on Route 66—and in Cincinnati, Ohio.

Home of the original chili burger

SAINT LOUIS SLINGER

Courtesy Diner on South King's Highway in Saint Louis serves close to one hundred slingers on a busy weekend night. Like the Eat-Rite (see page 105), the Courtesy Diner uses Edmonds Chile for their slinger.

SERVES 1

1 tablespoon unsalted butter

1 cup frozen shredded hash brown potatoes

1 (3-ounce) hamburger patty, cooked to desired doneness

2 eggs, fried or cooked in your preferred style

2 tablespoons finely chopped onions

1 cup Edmonds Chile or other mild chili with beans, heated

½ cup shredded cheddar cheese

2 slices toast, buttered

Melt the butter over medium heat in a 6-inch skillet; add the hash browns and pan-fry, turning once until crispy and browned on both sides. Spread the hash browns in a layer on a large plate or oval diner platter. Place the hamburger patty in the center of the hash browns. Slide the eggs over the hamburger. Sprinkle with raw onions. Cover the assembled potatoes, meat, and eggs with warm chili, then top with shredded cheese. Serve with the toast, cut diagonally into four pieces.

VARIATION

Breakfast Slinger Substitute 3 cooked strips of bacon or 2 cooked breakfast sausage patties for the hamburger patty.

ILLINOIS CHILLI WITH TWO "L'S"

This intensely flavored "Illinois chilli" recipe comes from Regional Chili Cook-off champion Les Estep of Rochester, Illinois.

SERVES 6 TO 8

4 ounces beef suet

3 pounds ground beef

1 white onion, chopped

3 celery stalks, chopped

1¼ cups chicken broth

1¼ cups beef broth

1½ cups tomato juice

1¼ cups water

1 teaspoon garlic powder

½ cup plus 1 tablespoon chili powder

½ teaspoon cayenne pepper, plus more to taste

1 tablespoon paprika

3 tablespoons ground cumin

1 teaspoon oregano

¼ teaspoon white pepper, plus more to taste

1 tablespoon brown sugar

2 (15-ounce) cans red kidney beans, with liquid

2 teaspoons salt, or to taste

In a large skillet or pot over medium-high heat, melt the suet and discard any remaining solids. Add the meat and lightly brown, 5 to 8 minutes. Add the onion and celery and continue cooking until softened, about 5 minutes. Add the chicken and beef broths, tomato juice, and water and reduce the heat to medium-low. Cover and simmer for 20 minutes.

Add the garlic powder, chili powder, cayenne, paprika, cumin, oregano, white pepper, and brown sugar. Reduce the heat to low, cover, and simmer for 2 hours.

Alternatively, transfer the chili to a slow-cooker and cook on low for at least 6 hours and up to 8 hours.

Skim the fat from the chili, if you desire. Add the beans and simmer uncovered for an additional 30 minutes, adding additional water as needed to prevent burning. Add salt to taste. You may wish to additionally adjust the spiciness to taste by adding additional white pepper and/or cayenne before serving.

POLLY BERGEN'S CHILI

This is the Walsh family chili recipe. My mom served chili often when I was growing up in Pittsburgh. My paternal grandfather was Irish-American and liked his chili over mashed potatoes, so that's the way Mom always served it.

When I asked her for her chili recipe while researching this book, she dug through her recipe card file and called me with an embarrassing confession. It turns out she had clipped Tennessee movie star Polly Bergen's chili recipe out of a magazine back in the 1950s. Mom made a few changes, but not many. Here then is a recipe for the Mary Ann Walsh/Polly Bergen chili I grew up on.

SERVES 12

3 cloves garlic, minced

2 tablespoons vegetable oil

6 large onions,
finely chopped

6 large green bell peppers,
finely chopped

6 pounds ground beef round

3 (16-ounce) cans
Italian-style tomatoes

2 (6-ounce) cans tomato paste

Salt and freshly ground
black pepper

2 teaspoons red wine vinegar

4 whole cloves,
wrapped in cheesecloth

3 bay leaves

¼ cups chili powder

3 pinches cayenne pepper

2 teaspoons ground cumin

4 (16-ounce) cans red
kidney beans, drained

In a large pot, over medium-high heat, sauté the garlic in the oil until light brown, then transfer to a bowl. Add the onions and peppers to the pot and sauté until the onions are golden; remove to the bowl with the garlic. Add the meat to oil in the large pot; separate with a fork and cook until all the meat is gray in color. Drain off the accumulated oil. Return the onions and green pepper to the pot; mix well and then add the tomatoes, tomato paste, salt, and pepper to taste, vinegar, cloves, bay leaves, chili powder, cayenne, and cumin.

Cover and simmer over low heat for 1 to 2 hours.

Alternatively, transfer the chili to a slow-cooker set on low and cook for for at least 6 and up to 8 hours.

Add the beans and cook for another 30 minutes. Remove the cloves and bay leaves before serving.

BRANSON CHILI CHEESE FRIES

The country music resort of Branson, Missouri, is a popular side trip on the cross-country Route 66 journey—it's about 50 miles south of the highway. And the best place to eat a bowl of chili in Branson is Gilley's Texas Café.

Gilley's was the enormous country music nightclub in Pasadena, Texas, made famous by the movie *Urban Cowboy*. Its founder now runs the Mickey Gilley Theater in Branson, Missouri, along with the café. Mickey Gilley markets his Wild Bull Chili Mix across the country (see wildbullcompany.com).

SERVES 4

2 pounds russet potatoes

2½ cups peanut oil

Salt

1 cup Gilley's Wild Bull Chili or favorite chili without beans, warmed

1 cup Slow-Cooker Chile con Queso (page 186), warmed

¼ cup pickled jalapeño slices

Peel the potatoes and cut into ½-inch sticks. Rinse and then pat dry with paper towels. Pour the oil into a 12-inch skillet. Add the potatoes, packing them in tight until the cold oil almost covers them.

Turn the heat to medium and cook the potatoes, shaking the pan to keep them from sticking, until they start to turn a pale golden color, about 10 minutes. Quit shaking the pan and cook for another 8 to 10 minutes until the potatoes begin to brown.

Increase the heat to medium-high and start turning the potatoes constantly, moving them around to ensure even browning. When evenly browned, drain and place on a wire rack. Sprinkle with salt.

To serve, divide the hot fries among four bowls and top with the chili con carne, then the chile con queso. Garnish with pickled jalapeño slices.

WALSH FAMILY "CHILI SIZE"

Start with 80/20 ground beef (80 percent beef to 20 percent fat) for a full-flavored burger patty. Cook them on a griddle if you want to emulate the Ptomaine Tommy's original—Dad cooked our burgers on the charcoal grill in the backyard.

You can use a Texas-style chili without beans instead of my Mom's Polly Bergen recipe, if you prefer. Dad liked his "chili size" without the bun.

SERVES 2

Salt and freshly ground black pepper

1 pound 80 percent lean ground beef chuck

1 teaspoon garlic powder

2 hamburger buns

2 pats butter

2 slices Colby, American, or other cheese

2 thin slices from a large sweet onion, such as Vidalia or Texas 1015

1 cup Polly Bergen's Chili (page 113)

Salt and pepper the meat, sprinkle with garlic powder, and knead to mix. When the spices are evenly spread, divide the meat into two equal portions and form into two patties. Cook the meat patties over medium heat on a griddle or gas grill or in a frying pan, turning several times. Resist the temptation to press down on the patty with the spatula—this squeezes out all the juices and results in a dry hamburger.

When the burgers are halfway done, split the buns and butter both sides. Lay the buns on the griddle or grill and toast them until they are nicely browned along the edges. Then place the buns on top of the burgers to steam. Half-pound burgers should be cooked to medium (150°F). After 12 to 15 minutes, check the level of doneness on a meat thermometer. When you have flipped the burgers for the last time, put the cheese slices on top.

When the meat patties are done and the cheese is melted, place the onion slice on the bottom buns and put the cheeseburger patties on top. Then put the chili on top of the patties and finish with the crown halves of the buns. Serve with a knife and fork.

VARIATION

Dad's Bunless "Chili Size" Prepare the meat patties as directed above, put the burgers topped with cheese in shallow bowls, cover with chili, and put the onion slices on top. Serve with a knife and fork.

CHILI WITH BEANS

"I like chili with beans. It makes it taste like a meal," Steven Ryan told me when I asked him about the "North of the Border" (chili with pinto beans) on the menu at Tolbert's Restaurant in Grapevine, Texas, where he is the manager.

"My grandfather would hate to hear me say that. Him and his friends were the ones who made the 'no beans' thing such a big deal."

Steven Ryan's grandfather, author, journalist, and chili cook-off impresario Frank X. Tolbert, was the leading advocate for what he called, "the world-famous, seldom-found-today, original, Texas-style bowl of red."

If you like beans in your chili, then by all means add some to the pot. But don't add canned or cooked beans to the chili too early in the cooking process; they get mushy and fall apart after an hour or so. And if you really love beans, consider cooking dried beans from scratch instead of using the canned varieties. You can substitute home-cooked beans (page 121) for canned beans in just about any recipe in this book.

Expand your legume horizons by trying some "heirloom beans." Ayocote negro, or black runner beans, mayocoba beans, cranberry beans, and black and white vaquero beans are just some of the varieties now available in specialty stores and from online sources. These older species of beans offer a variety of textures and tastes that make for an interesting change of pace in your chili cookery.

MOCK CHILI

The original Texas bowl of red was a meaty stew that became incredibly popular all across the country in the early twentieth century—but then things changed.

The Great American chili binge came to an abrupt halt in the 1940s. Wartime rationing limited the amount of meat families and restaurants could buy each week. In fact, supplies of meat were so limited that grocery stores had trouble stocking their meat cases.

Famous chili joints like Lang's in Dallas closed their doors during the war. Diners that had once served gallons of chili every day took it off the menu. Home cooks adapted with new recipes that stretched the meat with vegetables and starches. Like "mock duck" and "mock sausage," recipes for "mock chili" appeared in cookbooks and publications with advice to housewives on getting along with less meat.

After World War II, meat consumption was still restricted and the new version of chili persisted. Canned beans, canned tomatoes, canned corn, along with fresh green peppers, celery, and onions became normal ingredients for chili—the additions made the dish healthier, and eventually people just got used to it.

The ayocote negro is a large, shiny black bean that tastes even "meatier" than a kidney bean. It was very popular in Mesoamerica before the Spanish Conquest, according to heirloom bean expert Steve Sando.

Sando's company, Rancho Gordo, has launched a project to revive heirloom beans and help Mexican farmers by paying small farms in Mexico to grow the seldom-seen varieties for the gourmet market. The idea is to encourage biodiversity, save small farms in Mexico, and end up with a whole lot of interesting beans. (See www.ranchogordo.com.)

HOME-COOKED BEANS

If you like beans in your chili, cooking them at home instead of opening a can will yield better chili plus a flavorful bean broth. If you're in a hurry, you can cook soaked beans in a pressure cooker in around 20 minutes (the cooking time varies with the size, type, and age of bean). If want to cook them overnight or while you're at work, put them in a slow-cooker set on low, cover them with 3 inches of water, and cook for at least 6 hours and up to 8 hours.

A TENNESSEE BEANERY

Varallo's Chili Parlor, founded in 1907, is Nashville's oldest restaurant. Frank Varallo, Sr., a musician from Viggiano, Italy, brought a secret recipe for a spicy bean soup back from a performing tour of South America. After a hunting accident ended his career as a violinist, Varallo sold the fiery soup he called "chile" from a street cart in Nashville. At night, he set up the cart at a bar called the Climax Café. Eventually, "Frank the Chile King" became so famous he opened his own tavern.

Frank's great-grandson, Todd, runs the existing Varallo's location on Fourth Street in downtown Nashville. I met him at the restaurant for breakfast one morning. I ordered a dish called a "chile three-way." It was a bowl of white canellini beans cooked in a tomato sauce with short soggy spaghetti strands and a small tamale. The beans were cooked with a little meat, but not much. The dish didn't have any chile heat at all.

"The original Varallo's on Church Street was a tavern," Todd Varallo told me. "Spicy chile was good for business—after eating a bowl, customers drank a lot of beer." But the tavern location closed in 1998. The surviving Varallo's location is basically a downtown lunch room.

"We get a lot of families in here, and we don't sell any beer." So Todd Varallo took the cayenne out of his great-grandfather's recipe—all of it. "There is Louisiana hot sauce on the tables and crushed red pepper at the register if you want to make it hot," he apologized.

I think it's fair to say that Varallo's isn't really a chili parlor anymore, it has become what was once affectionately known as a "beanery."

CHAPTER 7
CONEYS AND THREE-WAYS: GREEK-AMERICAN CHILI TRADITIONS

Cincinnati chili parlors were inspired by the success of Greek restaurant owners in Detroit and elsewhere who were selling Coney Island hot dogs, or coneys, which were hot dogs topped with a Greek take on chili.

The first chili parlor in Cincinnati was opened on October 24, 1922, by Macedonian immigrants, Tom and John Kiradjieff, in a small corner storefront inside The Empress theater. The space held five marble-topped tables and a counter with stools. The menu consisted of coneys and spaghetti topped with chili—there was no cheese or other condiments. There was also a large pot from which coffee was served and a humidor full of local Ibold cigars.

John Kiradjieff at the original Empress Chili
(photo courtesy John Kiradjieff)

Just as chili thrived in the risqué environs of the red light district of San Antonio, it was right at home at The Empress theater where striptease acts were the main attraction. Across the river in Covington, Kentucky, vice had a different sort of spice—chili parlors there had illegal gambling dens in the back room.

In the spicy Greek ground meat stew called kima, the immigrants substituted cheap suet for the expensive olive oil, and added chili powder to the seasonings. The Americanized Greek stew was called "chili," to cash in on the popularity of the dish. Since the Greek kima used on the chili dogs was more or less the same as the topping for Greece's most popular spaghetti sauce, the Kiradjieff brothers added the Americanized version of Greek spaghetti topped with kima to their menu, creating what we now call "Cincinnati chili."

Many of the other famous Cincinnati chili chains were started by former employees of the Kiradjieff brothers and the restaurant chain that came to be called Empress Chili. Nicholas Sarakatsannis started Dixie Chili across the river in Covington Kentucky. And another Greek immigrant, Nicholas Lambrinides, left Empress in 1949 to start Skyline Chili, now the largest chain of chili parlors with more than 100 locations in the Tri-State area (Ohio, Kentucky, Indiana). In 2010, the Cincinnati chili industry had an estimated $159 million in sales.

THREE-WAYS AND FOUR-WAYS

"There are over 250 chili parlors in Cincinnati," Dann Woellert, the author of *The Authentic History of Cincinnati Chili*, told me. We met for lunch at Skyline Chili on Ludlow Avenue. Woellert ordered a "three-way," which means chili over spaghetti with onions, and I got a bowl of plain chili with oyster crackers and a cheese coney.

After reading Woellert's authoritative history and visiting a few old parlors, I confessed that I was awestruck by Cincinnati's chili culture. Like most Texans, I knew they had something they called chili here, but I wasn't prepared for its incredible popularity or the ardor of its fans.

In 2022, Ohioans will celebrate the one-hundred-year anniversary of Cincinnati chili.

"Cincinnati is the American chili capital," Woellert said with a smile, clearly enjoying a visiting Texan's bafflement. According to the Greater Cincinnati Convention and Visitors Bureau, Cincinnatians consume more than 2,000,000 pounds of chili each year, topped by 850,000 pounds of shredded cheddar cheese.

The cheese coney I was eating looked just like the ones at James Coney Island (now known as JCI Café), a hot dog chain opened by Greek immigrants more than ninety years ago in my hometown of Houston. The chili on the hot dogs and in my bowl tasted okay—except for the lack of chile pepper heat and the strangeness of the cinnamon.

It helped when Woellert explained that the unique style of Cincinnati chili seasonings were created by Macedonian immigrants who were borrowing from the Greek cuisine of their homeland. As I sampled my chili again, I realized that the cinnamon and allspice were reminiscent of the flavor of the meat mixture used in moussaka—a dish I like a lot.

A Greek immigrant told me that a visitor from Greece would instantly recognize Cincinnati chili as an American version of makaronia me kima (page 57). Somehow the realization that Cincinnati chili was an earnest attempt by hard-working immigrants to recreate a part of their culinary culture, rather than a messed-up version of Tex-Mex chili con carne, made the cinnamon-scented stuff in my bowl easier to enjoy. And after sampling a dozen or more examples, I have to admit, it started to grow on me.

Dan Wollert gave me a few tips about how to order and eat Cincinnati's favorite chili dishes. Swirling the spaghetti while eating a three-way is frowned on in Cincinnati, according to Woellert. The proper method is to cut down straight with a fork so that elements of all the layers are included in each bite.

A bowl of Cincinnati chili is properly served with cellophane packets of oyster crackers and pepper sauce on the side. Crushing the crackers into the bowl helps thicken the rather soupy style of chili and the hot sauce gives it a little bite.

The best spaghetti-and-chili dish I tried in the Cincinnati area was a special called a "Sriracha three-way" at a Gold Star Chili location in Covington, Kentucky. It was a bed of spaghetti topped with chili, Sriracha sauce, and cheese. The Asian-style hot sauce added a lot of zip to the otherwise bland pasta and meat sauce.

Of the Cincinnati chili chains, I was most partial to Gold Star, which also serves a passable bowl of Tex-Mex chili. In fact, the chain has a section of the menu dedicated to Tex-Mex. I had to order the monthly special, something called a "gorito." It was essentially a Frito Pie (with Tex-Mex chili) wrapped in a flour tortilla. It wasn't bad. It seems that Cincinnatians embrace all styles of chili; I was learning to do the same.

CHILI MAC

Chili with spaghetti is not a new idea, or a Cincinnati invention. It is known in most of the country as "Chili Mac." The recipe from the Mexene recipe booklet simply says: "Cook desired amount of spaghetti in usual way and fresh Chili con Carne seasoned with Mexene Seasoning—cook separately. Mix together when ready to serve in equal portions and serve hot." Chili Mac is not only a regular offering in United States military cafeterias, it is also one of the varieties of battlefield rations known as an "MRE" (Meal, Ready-to-Eat).

CONEYS AND TEXAS WEINERS

My family lived in Detroit for a few years when I was a little kid, but I could barely remember what a Detroit Coney tasted like. As luck would have it, while I was writing this book, I took a flight that was routed through Detroit. The layover was less than an hour, but I decided I could make it from gate A5 to the airport's only National Coney Island location at gate A51. I was a little winded when I sat down and ordered two coneys and a root beer.

The natural-casing hot dog made a satisfying snap when I took a bite. Enveloped in a soft steamed bun coated with brown mustard, smothered with thick chili and topped with chopped raw onions, my airport snack reminded me why Michiganers love their coneys so much. I barely made my connection—I was the last one on the plane. But I got my coneys.

There are some 387 Coney Island listings in the Michigan business phone directory. Regardless of the provenance the name suggests, the Coney Island hot dog (aka coney dog or coney) was created in Michigan, not Brooklyn, just as the Texas hot weiner, a regional deep-fried variant of the coney, hails from Altoona, Pennsylvania, not Texas. Both were invented within four years of each other, from 1914 to 1918. What they have in common—besides chili, frankfurters, mustard, and names that are geographical fantasies—are Greek immigrant inventors.

 A coney dog is a very specific regional variation on the generic chili dog. And of course, there are subgenres, including the Flint style and Jackson style, which replace the coney sauce with a dry ground meat topping, plus the "cheese coney," a shredded cheddar-topped coney variant popular in Cincinnati and Houston, among other places.

TEXAS HOT WIENER

Texas hot wieners were created in Altoona, Pennsylvania, by Peter "George" Koufougeorgas in 1918. The Paterson, New Jersey, version appeared sometime before 1920 and spread to Philadelphia. Altoona's original Texas Hot Dogs shop has two locations: downtown Altoona and 58th Street by the Logan Valley Mall. Paterson, New Jersey, still has several Texas weiner stands, including Libby's.

Also known as Texas hot dogs, Texas hots, or Texas wieners, these Greek-style chili dogs are favored on the East Coast.

In 1914, Greek immigrant George Todoroff founded what was probably the first of the coney stands in Jackson, Michigan. George's Jackson Coney Island was located in front of the Jackson train station on East Michigan Avenue. The menu was limited to Coney Island hot dogs, chili con carne, baked beans, pies, soft drinks, beer, and wine. The restaurant was open 24 hours a day, which made it popular with engineers, conductors, and train passengers. Four generations of Todoroffs ran the business over the years. Today the chain has been renamed Todoroff Original Coney Island.

The most influential chili dog stands in Michigan are the American Coney Island and Lafayette Coney Island restaurants located next door to each other in downtown Detroit. There is a fierce rivalry between the two—though, in fact, they were once related. American Coney Island was founded in 1917 by Greek immigrant Constantine "Gust" Keros. Gust brought his brother over from Greece and helped him open Lafayette Coney Island restaurant next door. The Keros family sold Lafayette Coney Island to its employees many years ago. American Coney Island seems to be winning the hot dog contest—the company's location in the D hotel in Las Vegas sells more coneys than the original in Detroit.

The sauce on coneys and Texas weiners are stretched with other ingredients like textured vegetable protein, cracker meal, or a white bread slurry. It tastes like a thick and meaty brown gravy with a hint of chili powder.

The original location of James Coney Island in downtown Houston

The spread of the chili dog is one the most important milestones in the history of chili. It was the early success of the Coney Island restaurants in Detroit and Texas weiner stands in the Northeast that encouraged a generation of Greek immigrants to try their hands at selling chili all over the country.

JAMES CONEY ISLAND

In the early 1900s, two carpenter's sons named Tom and James Papadakis left the Greek town of Kastelli and headed for America with little education and less money. The brothers eventually made their way to Houston, Texas, and, like many Greek immigrants of the era, decided to open a hot dog stand.

James Coney Island opened on Walker Street in downtown Houston in 1923. With 21 locations in the Houston area, James Coney Island—now known as JCI Cafe—is best known for its original coney with mustard, chili, and onions; and the cheese coney with mustard, chili, onions, and Kraft Cheez Whiz.

James Coney Island's chili is much more boldly seasoned than the Detroit version of coney sauce. JCI was one of the few eateries in Houston where you could always get a bowl of chili through the years. The restaurant also offers the locally beloved dish known as Frito pie (page 93). John Wayne, while in Houston to shoot the movie *Hellfighters*, became an ardent fan of JCI's chili.

The Papadakis family sold its interest in the chain to a group of investors in 1990, and the historic Walker Street location closed in 1993.

ORIGINAL CINCINNATI CHILI

The beef is never browned in authentic Cincinnati chili. The original recipe calls for beef, tallow, and water to be cooked together with onions and spices, then simmered for a long time until the chili reduces. This is essentially the same cooking method used by chuck wagon cooks in Texas (see Richard Bolt's "Deviled Beef," page 74). The water does the job of breaking up the beef. You can cook the chili uncovered if you want, but to avoid splattering it all over your kitchen, you probably want to partially cover the pot with a lid tipped to one side to let the steam escape.

SERVES 6 TO 8

½ cup beef tallow or
4 tablespoons vegetable oil

2 white onions, chopped

4 cloves garlic, chopped

2 pounds ground beef chuck

2 fresh or canned tomatoes, chopped

¼ cup apple cider vinegar

1 (15-ounce) can tomato sauce

½ teaspoon salt, or more to taste

½ teaspoon finely ground black pepper, or more to taste

¼ cup chili powder, homemade (page 11) or store-bought

2 tablespoons paprika

1 tablespoon ground cinnamon

2 tablespoons ground cumin

½ teaspoon ground allspice

¼ teaspoon ground cloves

Oyster crackers

Melt the tallow in a Dutch oven over medium-high heat. Add the onions and garlic and cook until the onion is softened, about 10 minutes. Add 4 cups of water and the ground beef, stirring to blend well. When the beef breaks up, add the tomatoes, vinegar, tomato sauce, salt, black pepper, chili powder, paprika, cinnamon, cumin, allspice, and cloves, stirring well.

Decrease the heat to a simmer and cook the chili for 1 hour or more.

Alternatively, transfer the chili to a slow-cooker set on low and cook for at least 6 and up to 8 hours. Adjust the seasonings to taste. Serve with oyster crackers.

CINCY CHILI LINGO

The unique nomenclature of Cincinnati chili (three-way, four-way, etc.) is part of American diner lingo—the shorthand invented by wisecracking waitresses to communicate with harried short-order cooks. Diner lingo also gave us such familiar terms as BLT (for bacon, lettuce, and tomato sandwich), O.J. (for orange juice), all the way (for a burger topped with lettuce, tomato, onion, pickle chips, mayo, and mustard) and Pittsburgh (to cook something until it is blackened).

CINCINNATI SPAGHETTI CHILI AND THE "WAYS"

Creamette brand spaghetti, which was once manufactured in East Saint Louis, is a favorite in Cincinnati, but almost any inexpensive American brand will do. To appreciate this all-American dish in its classic form, don't try to upscale it with imported Italian noodles or expensive English cheddar. And don't cook the pasta "al dente," the spaghetti under the chili in Cincinnati is thoroughly cooked.

SERVES 8

1 pound spaghetti

1 recipe Original Cincinnati Chili (page 128)

Cook the spaghetti according to the package directions, drain well, and divide among 8 large pasta bowls or lipped plates and top each portion with chili.

VARIATIONS

Three-Way Top each serving with 1 cup of finely shredded cheddar cheese.

Four-Way, Onion Sprinkle each serving with ½ cup chopped sweet onions, then 1 cup finely shredded cheddar cheese.

Four-Way, Beans Top each serving of spaghetti with ½ cup warm red kidney beans before adding the chili and 1 cup finely shredded cheddar cheese.

Five-Way Top each serving with ½ cup warm red kidney beans under the chili, ½ cup chopped sweet onions on top of the chili, and 1 cup finely shredded cheddar.

Six-Way Add an extra topping, such as fried garlic or pickled jalapeños to a Five Way.

Upside Down Any of the above constructed in reverse with the chili on the bottom.

HOMEMADE CONEY SAUCE

The recipe for the chili served at Greek hot dog stands is always kept a secret. The owner blends the spices according to a formula handed down by his ancestors. The truth is, you wouldn't want to know the secret recipe. Some include beef hearts and some include textured vegetable protein. Small Texas weiner stands in New Jersey ingeniously turn leftover hot dog buns into a slurry with water and use it to thicken their chili instead of using flour or cracker meal. There's nothing wrong with any of that—it's just not the way most of us cook at home.

Here's a homemade coney sauce recipe that you will probably like better than the real thing. When shopping for ground beef, look for meat that is finely ground. If you are grinding the beef at home, put it through the meat grinder twice using the 1/2-inch plate first and your smallest plate for the second grind.

MAKES SAUCE FOR
24 CONEYS

2 pounds finely ground ground beef chuck

1/2 cup tallow (or substitute solid white vegetable shortening, such as Crisco)

1 onion, minced

1 1/2 teaspoons chili powder, homemade (page 11) or store-bought

1 1/2 teaspoons paprika

1/2 teaspoon finely ground black pepper

1 teaspoon garlic powder

1 teaspoon ground cumin

3 bay leaves

2 teaspoons salt

In a large pot over medium-high heat, cover the beef and tallow with water and bring to a boil. Reduce to a simmer. With a potato masher, break up any clumps of meat, then simmer for 1 hour, covered, adding water as needed to maintain the desired consistency.

Mash again to break the meat into very small pieces. Add the onion, chili powder, paprika, black pepper, garlic powder, cumin, bay leaves, salt, and oregano; simmer for another 30 minutes. Remove the bay leaves and add the cracker meal. Stir and simmer for 20 more minutes, adding more water if necessary to achieve a smooth, pourable consistency.

VARIATIONS

Detroit-style Coney Sauce Eliminate the chili powder and proceed as directed.

Cincinnati-style Coney Sauce Add 1/2 teaspoon ground cinnamon and 1/4 teaspoon ground allspice with the rest of the spices and proceed as directed.

1 teaspoon dried
Greek oregano

1 cup cracker meal
(see page 74)

Houston-style Coney Sauce: Increase the chili powder to 2 tablespoons (or to taste) and proceed as directed.

CONEY KITS

American Coney Island is the most famous coney stand in Michigan. Their "coney kit" contains 12 Dearborn Sausage special recipe hot dogs, buns, a sweet onion, secret recipe Detroit coney sauce, instructions, and a hat. Kits start at $60 with shipping. (Americanconeyisland.com.)

Founded in 1965, National Coney Island has some sixty locations in Michigan. The chain sells a "coney kit" with a brick of their secret recipe frozen coney sauce, two dozen frozen hot dogs, two dozen buns, onions, and mustard. The cost is $40. (Nationalconeyisland.com)

DETROIT CONEYS

Detroit coneys start with a natural-casing all-beef hot dog. In Detroit coney stands, the hot dogs are authentically removed from the griddle or pan using a fork with the center tines removed. Never ask for ketchup or cheese on a coney in Detroit.

SERVES 12 (2 CONEYS EACH)

2 pats butter

24 top-quality hot dogs with natural casings

24 hot dog buns

Plochman's Yellow Mustard or another yellow mustard

Homemade Coney Sauce (page 132), heated

1½ cups grated sweet onion, such as Vidalia or Texas 1015

Melt the butter on a griddle over medium heat and arrange the hot dogs around it. Cook the dogs, turning often, until they are an even brown with black lines down two sides, 5 to 7 minutes. Remove from the griddle and set aside.

Steam the buns in nested Chinese steamers or wrap 3 buns at a time in a damp paper towel and microwave on high for about 20 seconds. Put a hot dog on each bun and add a stripe of mustard down each side. Cover with sauce, then sprinkle with onions, and serve.

Note Favorite hot dog brands in Detroit include Koegle, Dearborn, Sabrett, Kowalski, and Boars Head.

VARIATIONS

Cheese Coney Top the finished coney dog with ¼ cup shredded American or cheddar cheese and allow to melt a little before serving. Adding cheese to a coney is considered an abomination in Detroit, but in many other places, including Skyline Chili in Cincinnati and James Coney Island in Houston, cheese coneys are far more popular than the uncheesy ones.

Texas Wiener Deep-fry an all-beef hot dog and serve it on a steamed bun with Homemade Coney Sauce.

Texas Wiener All Day Top a Texas wiener with a squiggle of mustard and raw chopped onions.

CHAPTER 8

HALF-SMOKES AND ALL THAT JAZZ: AFRICAN-AMERICAN CHILI TRADITIONS

Ben's Chili Bowl is probably the most famous chili restaurant in the nation. Opened in 1958 in a former theater at 1213 U Street, Ben's is a DC landmark and an icon of the golden age of chili parlors.

Through the front window of the brightly painted historic building, you can see dozens of the fat half-smokes sizzling on the griddle. Inside, there is a line at the counter and a buzz of amiable mayhem as orders are shouted to the cooks. When it's my turn, I order a chili half-smoke with mustard, onions, and cheese; a bowl of chili; and a root beer.

A specialty of DC hot dog carts, a half-smoke sausage is fatter than a frankfurter, filled with a well-seasoned half-pork and half-beef mixture, and lightly smoked. It's very similar to the Polish sausage served in Chicago. The original was made by Briggs and Co., beginning in the 1930s.

Ben's signature dish, the original chili half-smoke is a 4-ounce link of the griddled sausage on a steamed bun, with mustard, onions, and chili sauce. The chili half-smoke was one the best "chili dogs" I've ever had. The meaty coarse-ground beef and pork link reminded me of that Texas barbecue tradition, Elgin sausage.

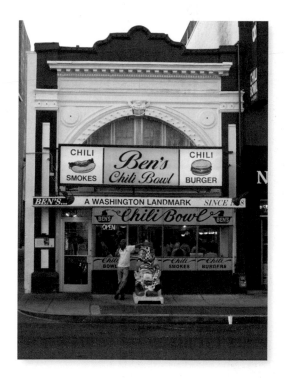

The chili came in a Styrofoam bowl with saltines. I asked for the cheese and onions on the side. The chili in the bowl had red kidney beans; it looked like a meaty gravy. The menu also features "all-meat" hot dogs and all-beef hot dogs served with chili. You can order chili con carne and vegetarian chili in various sizes topped with shredded cheddar.

Chili is popular in African-American cuisine, but there isn't really a monolithic soul-food chili style. While Gebhardt's set the standard ratio of 4 tablespoons (1 ounce) of chili powder to 2 pounds of meat, many soul-food chili recipes contain much less chili powder than that—particularly those from Northern cities. Miles Davis's chili mac calls for just 1 teaspoon.

African-Texan Hoover Alexander's favorite chili (see page 143) is hotter than the norm. Alexander, who worked as a line cook for the legendary Nighthawk Restaurant chain in Austin, Texas, now runs his own place, called Hoover's Cooking on Austin's Eastside—not far from the neighborhood where he grew up. He grows chile peppers in the restaurant's garden and makes fermented pepper sauces, which he sells at the restaurant. So, as you might expect, his chili is peppery.

So is Ben's chili, which calls for 5 tablespoons of chili powder per 2 pounds of meat. Ben Ali, the founder of Ben's Chili Bowl, whose full name is Mahaboob Ben Ali, was born in Trinidad and raised on fiery hot Indo-Trinidadian cuisine. There is a huge oil painting of the late Ben Ali on a wall in the interior second dining room of the restaurant. The rest of the walls are covered with likenesses of famous customers like Elvis Presley, George Bush, and a slew of foreign dignitaries that have visited Ben's Chili Bowl. French President Nicolas Sarkozy and his wife each had two of Ben's half-smokes during their visit to Washington, DC, in March 2010.

On my way home, I had another chili half-smoke at the Ben's Chili Bowl location inside Reagan Airport and, shockingly, the one at the airport tasted even better than the original.

MILES DAVIS'S SOUTH SIDE CHICAGO CHILI MAC

After eating chili mac in a Chicago soul-food shack, Miles Davis set out to copy the recipe. "I taught Frances how to make that dish, and after a while she was cooking everything better than me," he wrote after teaching his wife how to cook. Miles always wanted this chili mac after a three- or four-day binge, his wife reported. But Miles also had Frances serve it on important occasions, like a 1964 fundraiser for Robert Kennedy, where the guests included Bob Dylan, Quincy Jones, and Leonard Bernstein. Predictably enough, the host, Miles Davis, never showed up for the dinner.

SERVES 8

4 ounces suet

1 large onion

1 pound ground beef

½ pound ground veal

½ pound ground pork

Salt and freshly ground black pepper

2 teaspoons garlic powder

1 teaspoon chili powder

1 teaspoon cumin seeds

2 (15-ounce) cans kidney beans, drained

1 (10.75-ounce) can beef broth

1 drop red wine vinegar

1 pound spaghetti

Freshly grated Parmesan cheese and oyster crackers, for accompaniment

Heineken beer

Melt the suet over medium-high heat in large heavy pot; remove any remaining solids and discard. Add the onion and sauté until softened, about 3 minutes.

Combine the beef, veal, and pork in a bowl; season with salt, pepper, garlic powder, chili powder, and cumin seeds.

In another bowl, season the kidney beans with salt and pepper. Add the meat to the onion in the pot and sauté until brown, about 10 minutes. Add the kidney beans, beef broth, and vinegar; simmer for about 1 hour, stirring occasionally. Add more seasonings to taste, if desired.

Cook the spaghetti according to the package directions. Divide among eight plates. Spoon the meat mixture over each plate of spaghetti. Top with Parmesan and serve oyster crackers on the side.

Open the Heineken and drink.

JUST LIKE BEN'S CHILI

Ben's Chili Bowl gives out this recipe for chili—while it is no doubt slightly different from the original recipe, it's a close approximation.

SERVES 4

3 tablespoons vegetable oil

2 cloves garlic, minced

1 onion, chopped

5 tablespoons chili powder

2 teaspoons sugar

1 teaspoon ground cumin

2 pounds ground beef

¼ cup tomato paste

2 cups beef broth

6 tablespoons cornmeal

2 teaspoons salt

1 bay leaf

In a large pot over medium-high heat, heat the oil, then add the garlic and onion and sauté until golden, 7 to 9 minutes. Add the chili powder, sugar, and cumin. Cook, stirring constantly, for 2 more minutes. Add the ground beef and cook 5 to 7 minutes, stirring, until the beef is evenly browned. Stir in the tomato paste, beef broth, cornmeal, salt, and bay leaf. Reduce the heat to low and simmer for 15 to 20 minutes, until the chili is very thick. Discard the bay leaf before serving.

ORIGINAL CHILI HALF-SMOKES

If you can't find "half-smokes," use a natural-casing all-beef hot dog or smoked knockwurst.

**SERVES 12
(1 HALF-SMOKE EACH)**

Twelve ¼-pound half-smokes or all-beef frankfurters

12 hot dog buns

Yellow mustard

4 cups Just Like Ben's Chili (page 141)

2 cups shredded cheddar cheese

1 cup grated sweet onion, such as Vidalia or Texas 1015

Grill the sausages on a lightly greased griddle or large skillet over medium-high heat (or on a barbecue grill), then cut a split down the center. Remove from the heat and set aside. Steam the buns in nested Chinese steamers or wrap three buns at a time in a damp paper towel and microwave on high for about 20 seconds. Put a sausage on each bun and add a stripe of mustard down the split. Cover with the chili sauce, then sprinkle with cheese first, then onions.

Note You can order half-smoke sausages and other items from Ben's online store at benschilibowl.com/store.

HOOVER'S FREEZER CHILI

After family cookouts, Hoover Alexander saves any leftover cooked burgers and Elgin sausage and freezes them until he has a big enough batch to make chili. To start, he thaws out the meat and then grinds it coarsely in a food processor. He adds an important note: "Pre-seasoned [salted] burgers and the ratio of burgers to Elgin sausage or other meats [like breakfast sausage] will vary, so be sure to taste before you add more salt." He says to serve with cornbread and crackers.

SERVES 4

3 tablespoons vegetable oil

2½ cups chopped onion

3 tablespoons minced garlic

3 tablespoons minced jalapeño

2 pounds cooked leftover meats, such as hamburgers or sausage

5 cups water

¼ cup plus 1 tablespoon chili powder, homemade (page 11) or store-bought

2 tablespoons black pepper

1¼ teaspoons cayenne

2 teaspoons sugar

2 cups diced tomatoes

4 teaspoons paprika

2 tablespoons beef bouillon

¼ cup plus 2 tablespoons cornmeal

Salt, to taste

Chopped raw onion, to serve

Chopped jalapeño, to serve

In a large pot over medium heat, heat the oil, then add the onion, garlic, and jalapeños and sauté until the onions are translucent, about 5 to 7 minutes. Add the cooked meat and cook until heated through. Add the water, chili powder, pepper, cayenne, sugar, tomatoes, paprika, and bouillon, increasing the heat up to medium-high, and bring the mixture to a simmer. In a small bowl, mix the cornmeal with ¾ cup of the chili liquid, making a slurry. Add the slurry back into chili, stirring it in slowly. Turn flame to low and let simmer for 30 minutes. Serve garnished with the raw onion and jalapeño.

OBAMA FAMILY'S CHILI

President Barack Obama is an avid chili maker—it's about the only thing he cooks. When the president gave this recipe to *Good Morning America*, he noted: "I've been using this chili recipe since college and would bring it to any potluck. I can't reveal all the secrets, but if you make it right, it's just got the right amount of bite, the right amount of oomph in it, and it will clear your sinuses."

SERVES 4

1 large onion, chopped

1 green pepper, chopped

Several cloves garlic, chopped

1 tablespoon olive oil

1 pound ground turkey or beef

¼ teaspoon ground cumin

¼ teaspoon ground oregano

¼ teaspoon ground turmeric

¼ teaspoon ground basil

1 tablespoon chili powder

3 tablespoons red wine vinegar

Several tomatoes, depending on size, chopped

1 (15-ounce) can red kidney beans

White or brown rice, to serve

Accompaniments: Shredded cheddar cheese, chopped onions, and sour cream

Heat the olive oil in a large pot over medium-high heat and sauté the onion, green pepper, and garlic in the olive oil until soft. Add the ground meat and cook until browned. Combine the cumin, oregano, turmeric, basil, chili powder; add to the ground meat. Add the vinegar and tomatoes.

Let simmer until the tomatoes cook down, about 1 hour.

Alternatively, transfer the chili to a slow-cooker set on low and cook for at least 6 and up to 8 hours.

Add the kidney beans and cook for a few more minutes. Serve over white or brown rice. Garnish with shredded cheddar cheese, onions, and sour cream.

PART 4

MODERN AND VEGETARIAN CHILIS

CHAPTER 9

MODERN CHILI

Chili with black beans? Vegetarian chili? You've got to be kidding!" I said to the waiter at the Texas Chili Parlor in Austin as I looked over the menu. "Times change," he said with a shrug.

There was only one kind of chili on the menu when I started hanging out at this lovably funky old chili joint back in the 1970s. It was traditional Texas red, and it came in three heat levels—X, XX, and XXX. When you ordered XXX, they made you sign a hokey waiver of liability.

The look of the place hasn't changed a bit. The weathered wood exterior has giant shutters suspended by chains to keep the sun out. Inside there is a long bar (where I have spent many hours drinking Cuba Libres), and a little more than a dozen wooden tables, most with names or initials carved into them. The wood-paneled walls are covered with vintage enamel signs, beer neon, Terlingua chili cook-off memorabilia (see page 94), and a mounted deer head wearing a string of pearls.

While it may look like the same old Texas Chili Parlor, the menu has been drastically revised. Along with the X, XX, and XXX Texas reds that were once the stars of the menu, there is a selection of three other new-fangled chilis to choose from. I ordered a bowl of XX and all three of the new ones.

The Texas red was as good as ever. I think the recipe is very close to the Wick Fowler's Original Four Alarm Chili (page 96). Of the new additions, I liked the beef and Elgin sausage chili with black beans the best. It reminded me of race-car driver A. J. Foyt's chili recipe which contains some chorizo (page 89).

Elgin sausage is a spicy, coarse-ground all-beef sausage with a natural pork casing—it's been produced by the famous Southside Meat Market & Barbeque, a barbecue joint and butcher shop in the nearby town of Elgin, for over a hundred years. Cut-up links of Elgin's smoked sausage was a surprisingly brilliant addition to a bowl of chili.

I was also pleasantly surprised by the bright flavors in the green chile with pork, a stew of mild green New Mexican chiles thickened with masa harina and loaded with thin strips of tender white pork loin (page 41). The vegetarian three-bean chili with summer squash was a hearty bowl of beans with lots of spice, thickened with the squash.

If the Texas Chili Parlor in Austin, the last of the old-fashioned Texas chili joints, is serving vegetarian chili, then I think it's fair to say that the modern definition of chili has taken over in Texas. Of course, chili has been changing incrementally ever since William Gebhardt introduced his powdered seasonings. It got mixed up with beans in the Midwest, cinnamon in Cincinnati, and became a hot dog topping in Michigan.

With the new popularity of beef cuts like short ribs come new slow-cooking methods. You can use a slow-cooker for the long braising step when using short ribs (page 153) or a pot roast (page 151)—then cut up the braised-meat to make the finished chili. You'll be amazed by how great these braised meat chilis taste.

While venison and goat meat have long been considered suitable substitutes for beef in Texas chili con carne, turkey is a surprise. Substitute ground turkey (not the white meat-only variety, but the darker whole bird blend) for the ground meat in a quick-cooking chili recipe, and your family will swear they are eating beef.

Lamb is another seldom considered chili ingredient that is shockingly good. There is something about the gamey flavor of lamb that pairs very well with the bold spices of chili. And while Gebhardt gave a recipe variation for chili made with chicken way back in 1908, the relatively recent creation called "white chili" with chicken has become very popular in much of the Midwest.

There aren't any vegetarian chili recipes here—they have their own chapter (see page 165).

JAMES BEARD'S POT ROAST CHILI

James Beard classified chili as an appetizer and suggested filling little pastry shells with it as an hors d'oeuvre. But the "Chilied Pot Roast" recipe in James Beard's *American Cookery* has become one of my favorites. Instead of grinding or chopping a chuck roast and browning the meat, in this recipe, you braise the whole chuck roast in the chili mixture, then shred it and chop it after it has been cooked. Beard recommended hominy and flour tortillas with this dish—I prefer lightly mashed red potatoes and flour tortillas. The pot roast should be cooked until it is absolutely falling apart.

SERVES 6

2 dried ancho chiles, stemmed, seeded, and soaked in hot water

1 (3-pound) beef chuck roast

1 tablespoon salt

1 teaspoon black pepper

2 cloves garlic, cut in slivers

2 tablespoons tallow (see page 68)

2 onions, coarsely chopped

1 cup beef broth

1 (14.5-ounce) can stewed tomatoes

1 teaspoon dried Mexican oregano

1 teaspoon ground cumin

3 tablespoons New Mexican light red chili powder

Garnish: Chopped onion, fresh cilantro, and red serrano chiles

Boiled red potatoes, to serve

Heated flour tortillas, to serve

Remove the stems and seeds from the ancho chiles. Season the roast with salt and pepper. Pierce the meat with a knife in several places and insert the garlic slivers. Preheat the oven to 350°F or set out a slow-cooker large enough to cook the roast.

Heat the fat in a Dutch oven or large ovenproof braising pan over high heat. Add the roast and brown for 3 minutes on each side. Add the onions and cook until the onions are tender, about 5 minutes. Turn down the heat and add the broth, tomatoes, oregano, cumin and add the chiles and soaking liquid.

Braise in the oven for 3 hours, turning the meat over once every 30 minutes, until the meat is extremely tender.

Alternatively, transfer to a slow-cooker set on low and cook for 8 hours or more, until the meat is extremely tender.

Transfer the meat to a cutting board. Remove any gristle. Shred and chop the meat. Pour the remaining chiles and the braising liquid into a blender. Puree the chiles and liquid and return to the pot. Combine the meat and chile sauce.

Put the chili on the table in a bowl and garnish with chopped onion, cilantro, and red serranos. Serve with boiled red potatoes and flour tortillas on the side. To make tacos, roll up equal parts of chili and potatoes in flour tortillas.

TYLER FLORENCE'S SHORT RIB CHILI

If you don't braise beef short ribs long enough, they come out very tough. But it's hard to overcook them, so don't be in a rush. The slow-cooker is the easiest way to produce fork-tender, pull-apart ribs in a creamy, chocolate-spiked chile sauce. This rather elaborate recipe calls for several kinds of chiles and chili powders, designed to complement each other and round out the flavors. Serve over short pasta, potatoes, or risotto. Garnish with chopped onions and chopped cilantro, if desired.

SERVES 6

4 to 5 pounds square-cut, bone-in short ribs

Salt and freshly ground black pepper

2 tablespoons cumin seeds

1 tablespoon whole coriander seeds

¼ cup chili powder, homemade (page 11) or store-bought

2 tablespoons sweet paprika

2 tablespoons salt

1 tablespoon dried Mexican oregano

1 tablespoon sugar

1 tablespoon olive oil

2 onions, chopped

4 cloves garlic, minced

1 jalapeño chile, stemmed and chopped

3 canned chipotle chiles in adobo sauce, chopped

Preheat the oven to 325°F or select a slow-cooker large enough for the ribs. Generously season the short ribs with salt and pepper and set aside, keeping them at room temperature.

In a small skillet over medium heat, toast the cumin and coriander seeds separately. Toast for just a few minutes, shaking the skillet occasionally to prevent scorching. When the fragrance is released, transfer the toasted spices to a spice grinder and grind until the mixture is a fine powder. Transfer to a bowl and mix with the chili powder, paprika, salt, oregano, and sugar. Mix well and set the spice mix aside.

Add the oil to a Dutch oven over high heat and sear the short ribs on all sides. Transfer with tongs to a plate. Add the onions, garlic, and jalapeño to the Dutch oven the ribs were browned in, scraping to get up all the brown bits. Cook and stir until the onions have softened and turned translucent. Lower the heat to medium-low. Add the spice mix plus the chipotle in adobo. Stir to combine. Add the canned tomatoes, tomato paste, and chocolate. Use a wooden spoon or potato masher to break up the tomatoes. Return the ribs to the Dutch oven and coat with the tomato and spice mixture.

To cook in the oven, arrange the short ribs in the Dutch oven in a single layer if possible, making sure each one is completely coated in the chili mixture. Pour enough water over top to just cover the short

CONTINUED

1 (28-ounce) can
whole peeled tomatoes,
with their juice

1 tablespoon tomato paste

1 ounce Mexican chocolate

2 tablespoons masa harina
(optional)

ribs, 2 to 3 cups. Cover the Dutch oven securely, place in the preheated oven and cook for 3 or 4 hours, or until the ribs are completely tender and come off the bone.

To cook in a slow-cooker, combine the ribs and sauce in the cooker. Rinse the Dutch oven with 2 cups of water and pour over the ribs. Set the slow-cooker to high for 3 hours, then turn down to low and cook for 3 to 4 hours more, until the ribs are completely tender and the meat comes off the bone. (If you want to cook the ribs while you are at work or out of the house, just set the slow-cooker to low and let it go for 8 to 10 hours.)

Transfer the short ribs to a clean plate with tongs. Discard the bones, membrane, and excess fat. Use 2 forks to shred the meat from the ribs. Return the shredded meat to the pot and stir to combine with the cooking sauce. If the sauce is too thick, add water. If it's too watery, you can add some masa harina dissolved in water and let it cook for about 5 minutes on high to thicken. Taste and adjust the seasoning by adding salt and pepper to taste. Serve in a large bowl, family style.

BITTMAN AND BATALI'S LAMB CHILI

Mario Batali made lamb chili with harissa on television and called it Seattle Seahawks chili. Mark Bittman published a lamb and white bean chili recipe in the *New York Times*, remarking that the wonderful fragrance of lamb was perfect in chili. Here's a lamb chili adapted from the two recipes.

SERVES 4

2 tablespoons olive oil

1 pound ground lamb

Sea salt and black pepper

1 onion, finely chopped

4 cloves garlic, finely chopped

1 jalapeño chile, stemmed and finely chopped (seeds and all)

1 red bell pepper, stemmed, seeded, and chopped

4 poblano chiles, roasted (see page 19)

2 tablespoons chili powder (or more to taste)

1 teaspoon ground coriander

2 teaspoons ground cumin

1½ tablespoons tomato paste

4 cups water

1½ cups cooked cannellini beans, homemade (page 121) or canned

1½ cups cooked red kidney beans, homemade (page 121) or canned

2 cups cooked brown rice

Plain yogurt, for serving

Heat the oil in a Dutch oven over medium-high heat. Add the lamb and cook, breaking up with a fork, until well browned, 5 minutes. Season with 1 teaspoon each salt and pepper, or more to taste. Transfer the meat to a bowl.

Add the onion to the pot, stirring to get all the lamb bits. Cook until the onion is softened, about 5 minutes. Stir in the garlic, jalapeño, and red pepper and cook for 2 minutes. Dice 3 of the poblanos and add, along with the chili powder, coriander, and cumin, and cook for 1 minute. Stir in the tomato paste and cook until it begins to turn brown. Return the lamb to the pot. Stir in the water and beans. Simmer over medium-low heat for 45 minutes; add more water if the chili becomes too thick. Taste and adjust seasonings, if necessary.

To serve the chili, put ½ cup of the rice in each of four bowls. Divide the chili among the four bowls. Cut the remaining roasted poblano into neat strips. Garnish each bowl of chili with a dollop of yogurt and top with crisscrossed poblano strips.

ROBERT REDFORD'S LAMB CHILI WITH BLACK BEANS

This lamb chili recipe first appeared in Paul Newman's *Newman's Own Cookbook* published in 1998. I made a few minor alterations, like specifying olive oil and substituting fresh mint for the dried stuff. No doubt the Sundance Kid would want you to use Colorado lamb and New Mexican pine nuts.

SERVES 3

1½ pounds lamb stew meat, cut into 1-inch cubes

½ cup olive oil

6 cloves garlic

½ red onion, diced

2 tablespoons chili powder

1 tablespoon ground coriander

3 large tomatoes

4 cups chicken broth

1 (16-ounce) can crushed tomatoes

2 tablespoons tomato paste

1 tablespoon Worcestershire sauce

1½ cups cooked black beans

1 pinch chopped fresh mint

Salt and black pepper

Chopped white onion, to garnish

Chopped green onion, to garnish

Sour cream, to garnish

½ cup toasted pine nuts, to serve

Marinate the lamb chunks in the oil, with the garlic, red onion, chili powder, and coriander for a few hours.

Blacken the tomatoes in a dry cast-iron skillet over medium-high heat, turning to scorch all sides. Remove the tomatoes from the pan, remove any loose skin, chop them coarsely, and set aside.

Drain some of the oil from the lamb into a Dutch oven and heat over medium-high heat until the oil sizzles. Add the lamb and the rest of the marinade and cook for 5 minutes, stirring to brown the meat. Add the blackened tomatoes, chicken stock, crushed tomatoes, tomato paste, and Worcestershire sauce. Bring to a boil, then turn the heat to medium-low and cook, stirring occasionally, for 35 minutes. Add the beans, mint, and salt and pepper to taste. Stir often to prevent scorching and cook for another 10 minutes.

Serve the chili in large bowls garnished with onions, green onions, and sour cream. Pass the pine nuts separately.

COCOA BIRD CHILI

The flavor of the unsweetened chocolate might remind you of mole, a favorite sauce with turkey and chicken in Mexico. Avoid buying white meat–only ground turkey or ground chicken for this recipe. You want lots of flavorful dark poultry meat in this hearty chili.

SERVES 8 TO 10

1 tablespoon vegetable oil

2 onions, chopped

2 cloves garlic, chopped

1½ teaspoons dried oregano

1½ teaspoons ground cumin

1 pound ground dark meat turkey

1 pound ground chicken

¼ cup chili powder

2 bay leaves

1 tablespoon unsweetened cocoa powder

1½ teaspoons salt

1 (28-ounce) can whole tomatoes

3 cups chicken stock

1 (8-ounce) can tomato sauce

1½ cups cooked cannellini beans, homemade (page 121) or canned and drained

1½ cups cooked red kidney beans

Chopped red onion, to serve

Chopped fresh cilantro, to serve

Sour cream, to serve

Heat the oil in a Dutch oven over medium heat. Add the onions and sauté until light brown and tender, about 10 minutes. Add the garlic, oregano, and cumin; stir for 1 minute. Increase the heat to medium-high. Add the turkey and chicken; stir until no longer pink, breaking up the meat with back of a spoon. Stir in chili powder, bay leaves, cocoa powder, and salt. Add the tomatoes with their juices, breaking up the tomatoes with the back of a spoon. Mix in the stock and tomato sauce. Bring to a boil. Reduce the heat; simmer for 45 minutes, stirring occasionally.

Add the beans to the chili and simmer until the flavors blend, about 10 minutes longer. Discard the bay leaves before serving.

To serve, ladle the chili into bowls. Pass the red onion, cilantro, and yogurt separately.

WHITE CHICKEN CHILI

Kansas City seems to be the birthplace of "white chili." This is an adaptation of the first recipe in print from the cookbook *Beyond Parsley: Beautiful Food* (1984) by the Junior League of Kansas City, Missouri. Serve topped with Jack cheese.

SERVES 4

1 tablespoon butter

1 tablespoon olive oil

3 boneless skinless chicken breasts, cut into ½-inch pieces

2 white onions, chopped

3 large cloves garlic, minced

3 tablespoons all-purpose flour

1 pickled jalapeño chile, chopped

¼ teaspoon cayenne pepper

1 teaspoon dried oregano

2 teaspoons ground cumin

4 cups chicken broth

4 ounces canned green chiles, freshly roasted green Anaheim, or New Mexico long green chiles (page 19), chopped

3 (14.5-ounce) cans cannellini (white kidney) beans, rinsed and drained

½ teaspoon salt

½ teaspoon white pepper

1 cup shredded Jack cheese, for topping

In a Dutch oven, heat the butter and oil over medium heat. Add the chicken and sauté until cooked through. Remove the chicken with a slotted spoon and set aside. Add the onions and garlic and cook until softened and translucent. Reduce the heat to low and sprinkle the flour over the onion mixture, stirring to coat. Stir in the pickled jalapeño, cayenne, oregano, and cumin. Add the chicken broth, the chicken, chopped green chiles, and cannellini beans. Add the salt and white pepper. Increase the heat to medium-high and bring the chili to a boil; reduce the heat to low and cook for 10 minutes. Serve family style in a large bowl topped with shredded cheese.

WHITE CHICKEN POBLANO CHILI

Here's a more satisfying version of white chicken chili in which you cook a whole chicken instead of using boneless breasts and create your own chicken stock in the process. Poblano chiles can vary in heat intensity from very mild to medium-hot. This recipe calls for seeded and stemmed fresh chiles, but if you like more heat, just remove the stem and leave the seeds and the white membranes intact.

SERVES 6 TO 8

1 whole chicken,
cut into 8 pieces

10 cups water

2 tablespoons butter

2 tablespoons olive oil
or vegetable oil

1 white onion, chopped

4 large cloves garlic, minced

6 to 8 poblano chiles, roasted
(see page 19)

1 jalapeño chile, seeded,
stemmed, and thinly sliced

1 pound dried Great Northern
beans, rinsed and soaked in
water for 2 to 3 hours

½ teaspoon chili powder

½ teaspoon cayenne pepper

1½ tablespoons ground cumin

2 tablespoons masa harina

1 cup whole milk

½ teaspoon salt, or to taste

White pepper

Sour cream, to garnish

Put the chicken in a stockpot over medium heat and add the water. Bring to a boil, then lower the heat and simmer until the chicken is cooked through, 20 to 30 minutes. Remove the chicken with a slotted spoon, set aside, and allow to cool. Reserve the broth and add water, if necessary, to yield 8 cups. Remove the skin from the chicken and discard. Then remove the meat from the bones—you should have about 3 cups of cooked chicken.

In a Dutch oven over medium heat, heat the butter and oil. Add the onion and garlic and cook until softened, about 8 minutes, being careful not to brown the vegetables. Reserve 1 poblano for the garnish and cut it into long, thin strips. Chop the remaining poblanos and add to the pot along with the sliced jalapeños and drained soaked beans. Add the chili powder, cayenne, and cumin.

Add the chicken broth and cook for 1 hour. Add the chicken and continue cooking for another hour, until the beans are fully cooked.

Alternatively, transfer the chili to a slow-cooker set on low and cook for at least 6 and up to 8 hours.

When the beans are thoroughly cooked, dissolve the masa harina in the milk and add to the pot. Cook for an additional 15 minutes on high, and add salt and white pepper to taste.

Serve garnished with sour cream and the reserved roasted poblano chile strips.

CHAPTER 10

VEGETARIAN CHILI

If chili is a tanglesome topic, then vegetarian chili is a particularly thorny snarl within the larger briar patch. The very idea of vegetarian chili makes some people mad. While much is made about the debate over beans versus no beans, that's a minor squabble among close friends compared to the vicious dispute over meat versus no meat.

Vegetarian chili might seem like a recent invention, but in fact, it was in the news during World War I. Herbert Hoover, head of the United States Food Administration (USFA), came up with the campaign for "Meatless Monday" to encourage American families to cut consumption of meat to support American troops and help feed our allies at a time when German U-boat campaigns forced the rationing of meat and sugar in Britain.

Some 13 million American families signed the Meatless Monday pledge, and meat consumption in America declined by around 15 percent. President Franklin D. Roosevelt revived Meatless Monday during World War II, and it was continued by his successor, Harry S. Truman, as part of the post-war campaign to help Europeans.

In 2003, Meatless Monday was reintroduced by health food activists who believe Americans eat too much meat. Meatless Monday was adopted by the Baltimore public school lunch program in 2009. Other municipalities have proposed similar cafeteria menus.

ANOTHER CHILD OF MRS. NECESSITY— IT'S MEATLESS CHILI

"Firm Roberts, rotund dispenser of newspapers, magazines, hot dogs, chili, and confections, being of a patriotic disposition, set his creative mind to working upon reading the new food law regarding the meatless and wheatless day, and yesterday 'Firm' let ye scribe partake of some of the new chili sans meat and b'lieve us, it is good! This fact is corroborated by 98 others of the first 100 customers served yesterday said it was better than the regular chili.

Yesterday's customers were so well pleased that Firm states he is going to serve his 'Creole Chili' every day and discontinue the making of his old style chili.

Another thing, we report. Firm says that no living person except himself knows the ingredients used in this 'Patriotic Creole Chili' and consequently he will be the only one in Columbus to serve 'law-abiding chili' on meatless days. The chili is warranted to be pure, wholesome and refreshing."

—*Columbus (Ohio) Enquirer-Sun*, February 20, 1918

As my credentials are somewhat suspect in the meatless chili department, I was aided in developing recipes for this chapter by a bona fide vegetarian chili enthusiast, my daughter Katie Walsh. Katie is a food blogger and herbalist who explores healthy alternatives to conventional cooking in her writing.

In an interesting discussion on vegetarian chili on the Serious Eats website, editor Kenji Lopez-Alt elaborated on his aversion to meat analogues in vegetarian dishes. Kenji also had a great suggestion about flavorings. Marmite (a by-product of brewing that is essentially yeast extract) and soy sauce are *"packed* with glutamates" in his words. And glutamates are an excellent way to conjure up meaty umami flavors.

Umami, the fifth flavor, can turn vegetarian chili into a satisfying meal. Along with Marmite and soy sauce, vegans rely on mushrooms, seaweed, and other glutamate-rich ingredients to give a pot of vegetable chili a boost.

On the subject of meat substitutes, Katie disagreed with Kenji: Bean chilis are fine, but there is no real reason to avoid tempeh, seitan, or tofu in a dish that was originally dominated by meaty proteins.

If vegetarian chili is up your alley, I think you'll be pleased with the recipes here. There is nothing wimpy about these chilis when it comes to the heat levels. And if you never cooked vegetarian chili in your life, maybe this would be a good time to surprise someone you know with chili next Meatless Monday.

CHILI SIN CARNE

In the style of classic chili con carne, this meat-free chili is hearty with no-frills. It has a purely chile-based sauce with no tomato and is made with raw chocolate and ground seitan, a "wheat meat" made of gluten and thought to have originated in ancient China for the vegetarian Buddhist monks. Serve over veggie enchiladas, with chips, or sop it up with tortillas. Don't forget the diced onions and shredded cheese!

SERVES 6

4 dried ancho chiles

2 dried chipotle chiles

4 dried New Mexican long red or guajillo chiles

2 tablespoons extra-virgin olive oil

2 onions, chopped

3 large or 6 small cloves garlic, minced

2 (8-ounce) packages ground seitan

1 tablespoon sea salt

2 tablespoons sweet paprika

½ teaspoon ground allspice

1 teaspoon ground cumin

2 tablespoons raw cacao powder (unprocessed cocoa)

4 cups vegetable broth

1 tablespoon masa harina

Tear the chiles in half and discard the stems and easily removed seeds. Toast the chiles in a dry skillet over medium heat until warm and aromatic, 2 to 3 minutes each side. Turn off the heat and transfer the chiles to a small saucepan and cover with water. Press them down into the water so that they're mostly submerged. Heat the water over medium heat for a few minutes, then turn off the burner. Do not boil.

Heat 1 tablespoon of the oil in a heavy saucepan or Dutch oven over medium heat. Add the onions and cook for 5 minutes, stirring occasionally, then add garlic and cook another 5 minutes. Transfer the cooked veggies to a high-powered blender or food processor.

Add the remaining 1 tablespoon oil to the pan and crumble the seitan into it. Add the salt, paprika, allspice, cumin, and cacao and stir well. Brown the seitan over medium heat for about 10 minutes, stirring occasionally.

Meanwhile, drain the chiles, coarsely chop, and add to blender with 1 cup of the soaking liquid. Puree on high until very smooth.

Pour the chile puree into the Dutch oven with the browned seitan and add the vegetable broth. Bring to a boil and stir in masa harina dissolved in water, then reduce to low and cook, uncovered, until thickened, about 1 hour.

FIVE-CHILE TEMPEH CHILI

This is a hearty veggie chili made with tofu's cousin tempeh, a less-processed fermented soybean product with a nutty flavor and texture. Don't be alarmed if you see spots on it when you open the package; it's not moldy, it's supposed to look like that.

The dish resembles calabacitas, a Tex-Mex dish in which summer squash is cooked down into a thick sauce. Mexican spices, calabacitas, and five different chiles make this a spicy chili-calabacitas hybrid. Serve with cornbread (page 185) or by itself.

SERVES 12

1½ cups dried black beans, soaked overnight and drained

6 large tomatoes, or 12 plum tomatoes

2 tablespoons olive oil, plus more as needed

1 onion, chopped

2 cloves garlic, minced

2 stalks celery, chopped

3 large carrots, chopped

1 jalapeño chile, chopped (with seeds)

1 pound tempeh, cubed

1½ teaspoons ground cumin

2 teaspoons sea salt

1½ teaspoons dried Mexican oregano

3 cups chopped summer squash (or substitute zucchini)

In a large pot of water over high heat, boil the beans until just tender, about 1 hour. Take the pot of beans off the heat.

Stem the tomatoes, cut small Xs in their bottoms, and blanch in a large pot of just-boiling water for a few minutes until the skins blister. Transfer with a slotted spoon to an ice bath to loosen the skins, about 1 minute. Gently pull the skins away from the flesh of the tomatoes and discard the skins.

In a Dutch oven over medium-high heat, heat the olive oil and add the onion, garlic, celery, carrots, and jalapeño; sauté until slightly softened, about 5 minutes. Stir in tempeh, cumin, salt, and oregano and add just enough additional oil as needed to coat well (but not pool at the bottom). Sauté until the tempeh is golden brown, about 10 minutes. Reduce the heat to medium-low and stir in squash and poblanos. Cover and continue to cook until the squash is brightened in color, about 3 minutes.

Use your hands or a potato masher to crush tomatoes and add them and their juices into the pot. Stir in the V8 juice and chile powders. Simmer on medium low, uncovered, for 20 minutes.

2 poblano chiles, roasted
(see page 19) and cut
into 1-inch squares

12 ounces V8 or tomato juice

2 tablespoons ancho
chile powder

2 teaspoons chile de
arbol powder

1 tablespoon chili powder,
homemade (page 11)
or store-bought

Kernels cut from
1 ear fresh corn

Salt and freshly ground
black pepper

1 tablespoon Marmite
(optional)

Add the beans plus 1 cup of their soaking liquid and continue simmering the chili until the beans are very soft, 45 minutes to 1 hour. Stir in the corn kernels and cook an additional 10 minutes. Add salt and pepper to taste and the Marmite, if desired. Serve with saltines.

THREE-BEAN CHIPOTLE CHILI

A pot of slow-cooked beans tastes fabulous with the rich, smoky flavor of chipotle chiles. Pass chopped green onions and lime wedges for a garnish.

SERVES 6 TO 8

⅓ pound dried coloradito or red kidney beans

⅓ pound dried pinto beans

⅓ pound dried garbanzo beans

1 tablespoon extra-virgin olive oil

1 onion, chopped

2 large or 4 small cloves garlic, minced

1 tablespoon sea salt

1 teaspoon ground cumin

1 tablespoon chili powder, homemade (page 11) or store-bought

½ teaspoon dried Mexican oregano

1 bunch green onions, bulbs and greens chopped (reserve some greens for garnish)

1 (3.5-ounce) can chipotle chiles in adobo sauce

1 (28-ounce) can diced tomatoes

4 cups vegetable broth

Soak the beans overnight. Heat the oil in a Dutch oven over medium heat and sauté the onion until slightly soft, about 5 minutes. Add the garlic and cook until the onions are translucent and beginning to brown, another 3 minutes. Add the salt, cumin, chili powder, and oregano and stir to incorporate.

Drain the beans and add with the green onions, chipotles, tomatoes, and broth and bring to a boil, then reduce heat and cover. Cook until the beans are tender and chili has reached desired consistency, about 3 hours.

Alternatively, transfer to a slow-cooker set on low and cook for at least 6 and up to 8 hours, then serve.

BORRACHO BLACK BEAN CHILI

This thick, sultry black bean chili gets a kick from a bottle of Negro Modelo beer, which makes it a "borracho," or drunken chili. Eat it as a main dish with crushed tortilla chips and sour cream on top or a piece of crusty bread, or serve it as a side with tamales, tacos, or a steak.

SERVES 10 TO 12

1 pound dried black beans

1½ tablespoons sea salt

1 onion, chopped

2 large or 4 small cloves garlic, minced

1 large red bell pepper, chopped

2 small green bell peppers, chopped

1 large jalapeño, chopped with seeds (for mild chili, remove seeds)

2 tablespoons chili powder, homemade (page 11) or store-bought

1 teaspoon dried Mexican oregano

½ teaspoon ground cumin

1 teaspoon freshly ground black pepper

1 (12-ounce) bottle Negro Modelo (or other dark beer)

1 (6-ounce) can tomato paste

Soak the beans overnight. Drain the beans and discard the soaking liquid, pour into a soup pot, and cover with 6 cups fresh water. Add 1 tablespoon salt, cover, and bring to a boil. Reduce to a simmer and cook until beans are tender, about 1½ hours.

Add the onion, garlic, red and green peppers, jalapeño, remaining ½ tablespoon salt, chili powder, oregano, cumin, and black pepper. Stir well, then slowly pour in the beer. Add the tomato paste and stir well until totally dissolved.

Continue cooking over low heat, uncovered and stirring occasionally, until the liquid level reduces down to expose a layer of beans, 45 to 60 minutes. Taste and adjust seasoning as desired, then serve.

LENTIL, SWEET POTATO, AND ANCHO CHILI

One of the hardest things about vegetarian chili is getting the consistency right: it's hard to achieve the ideal gravy-to-chunk ratio. This lentil and sweet potato version gets very close—the secret is pureeing half the stew and adding it back in as a thickener. Fresh ginger, garlic, and basil sautéed in butter and a pinch of cinnamon and allspice give it some zing.

SERVES 10 TO 12

1 pound dried green lentils, soaked for 4 to 6 hours then drained

1 large sweet potato, chopped (do not peel)

1 pound tomatoes, chopped

1 tablespoon sea salt

1 tablespoon sweet paprika

½ teaspoon cayenne pepper

½ teaspoon ground cinnamon

¼ teaspoon ground cloves

4 cups vegetable broth

3 dried ancho chiles

½ tablespoon butter

2 large or 4 small cloves garlic, chopped

1-inch piece fresh ginger, peeled and chopped (about 1 teaspoon)

6 leaves fresh basil

Put the lentils, sweet potato, tomatoes, salt, paprika, cayenne, cinnamon, and cloves into a Dutch oven. Cover with the broth, cover the Dutch oven, and bring to a boil over medium-high heat, stirring occasionally. Reduce the heat to a simmer and cook until the sweet potatoes are tender, about 1½ hours.

Tear the anchos in half and discard the stem and easily removed seeds. Toast the anchos in a dry skillet over medium heat until warm and aromatic, 2 to 3 minutes each side. Turn off heat and transfer chiles to a small saucepan and cover with water. Press them down into the water so that they're mostly submerged. Heat the water over medium heat for a few minutes, then turn off the burner. Do not boil.

In a small frying pan, melt the butter over medium heat. Add the garlic and ginger and cook until fragrant, about 1 minute. Stir in fresh basil leaves and wilt for about another minute. Remove from the heat.

Once the sweet potatoes are tender, ladle about half of the solid ingredients (about 4 cups) into a high-powered blender or food processor, allowing most of the liquid to drain back into the pot before transferring. Drain the softened anchos. Chop coarsely and add to the blender along with ginger and garlic mixture. Puree until very smooth and thickened; the mixture should be a thick paste.

Use a rubber spatula to return the paste to the pot and stir well to integrate completely. Continue simmering over low heat for about 15 minutes to combine flavors. Taste and adjust seasoning. Serve in a bowl, family style.

GREEN CHILI

The tomatillos make it tart, the zucchini melts into the sauce, the broccoli adds a chunky texture, and the chiles bring a whole lot of zip. This tastes great with fresh corn tortillas and an omelet.

MAKES 6 SERVINGS

1 pound tomatillos, husked and rinsed (about 8)

2 fresh serrano chiles

1 large fresh poblano chile

1 bunch fresh cilantro

Juice of 1 lime

1 teaspoon honey

2 tablespoons butter

1 large red onion, chopped

3 large or 6 small cloves garlic, minced

2 zucchini, chopped (about 3 cups)

1 head broccoli, florets and tender part of stem, chopped (about 3 cups)

1 tablespoon plus 1 teaspoon sea salt

1 teaspoon black pepper

1 teaspoon ground cumin

1 teaspoon dried Mexican oregano

2 cups vegetable broth

Sliced avocado, to serve

Toasted pumpkin seeds, to serve

Cover the tomatillos with water in a saucepan, cover, and bring to a boil. Remove the lid, reduce the heat, and boil until they become softened and dull in color, about 15 minutes.

Meanwhile, roast the serrano and poblano chiles in a dry frying pan over medium-high heat, rotating periodically to blister the skin on all sides, about 10 minutes. Remove from the heat, seal in a plastic bag, and once cool enough to handle, remove the stems.

Drain the tomatillos and transfer to a high-powered blender or food processor along with serranos, poblano, cilantro, lime juice, and honey. Puree until smooth.

Heat the butter in a heavy pot or Dutch oven over medium heat. Add the red onion, garlic, zucchini, broccoli, salt, pepper, cumin, and oregano and stir to coat evenly. Cook until the zucchini is softened, 12 to 15 minutes.

Add the tomatillo puree and broth to the pot and bring to a boil. Reduce the heat to a simmer and cook, uncovered, until the liquid is reduced by half and the chili reaches a desired consistency, about 1 hour.

Serve with slices of avocado and toasted pumpkin seeds on top.

HOW TO THROW A CHILI PARTY

My family's traditional Halloween dinner is a chili buffet. Slow-cookers are filled with chili con carne, chile con queso, beans, and tamales. There are big bowls full of tortilla chips and individual bags of Fritos, plus condiments including shredded cheese, chopped raw onions, and sour cream. An impromptu party usually develops as the neighbors stop by on their trick-or-treat rounds.

It's such an easy way to feed a crowd that we also started putting out the chili buffet when the team stops by after the Little League game, for football-watching gatherings on Saturday and Sunday afternoons, and for casual occasions over the rest of the year. But after a few of these get-togethers, I realized I needed to come up with some new chili dishes so I wasn't serving my friends the same stuff every time.

I was looking for inspiration when I discovered the Hard Times Café chain in Washington, DC. Hard Times is the United Nations of chili, and I can't think of a single chili dish that doesn't appear on their menu—there are also several I had never heard of before.

Fred Parker opened the first Hard Times restaurant in Alexandria, Virginia, in 1980. It was an homage to Hazel's Texas Chili Parlor, a 1960s-era Washington, DC, cafe that was located in a tough neighborhood in the 1900 block of Pennsylvania Avenue near the bus station. Parker fondly remembered Hazel's as an outpost of the Old West in downtown DC. There was a green neon cactus in the window,

HARD TIMES CHILI DISHES

- Texas, Terlingua, Cincinnati, or Vegetarian Chili
- Bowl of chili with choice of condiments (onion, cheese, sour cream) and a basket of saltines and oyster crackers
- Bowl of chili with beans
- Chili over rice
- Quarter pound all-beef chili dog
- Coney dog with or without cheese
- Chili cheese fries
- Extra-large tower of chili nachos
- Frito pie
- Chili mac featuring spaghetti with any chili in the house
- 3-way (chili, spaghetti, and cheese)
- 4-way (chili, spaghetti, onions, and cheese)
- 5-way (chili, spaghetti, onions, beans, and cheese)
- Chili Bubba (two kinds of chili over cornbread with cheese, onions, and sour cream)
- Chili Taters (a bowl of tater tots smothered with chili, cheese, and sour cream)
- Chili burger

Hank Williams on the jukebox, and a colorful crowd seated at a long bar—the place was open until 3 a.m.

Hazel's chili was a simple Texas blend of chopped beef, garlic, onions, and tomatoes simmered in suet and seasoned with chili powder and cumin. One of Hazel's most famous offerings was chili mac: "all the way, wet." To make the signature dish, chili was ladled over spaghetti and topped with California pink beans, onions, and Parmesan. The "wet" part was an extra spoonful of the molten orange suet that floated on top of the chili pot.

Although the menu has expanded to include a cornucopia of chili specialties, the original Texas chili at Hard Times is remarkably close to Hazel's original. Over the years, requests from bean lovers, Frito pie fanciers, Cincinnati 3-way eaters, and Michigan coney fans have prompted the slow evolution of Hard Times Café from a simple Texas-style chili joint to a showcase of American chili styles, fittingly located in the nation's capital.

For all those provincial chili fans who find it necessary to denigrate the chili of other places for bizarre seasonings, legume inclusions, spaghetti beds, and other regional quirks, Fred Parker provides a much-needed role model. He encourages us to confront our long history of chili con carne xenophobia.

Reading his Hard Times menu with its array of chili specialties from all over the country, you have to wonder: "Can't we all just get along?"

SETTING UP A CHILI BUFFET

The easy way to pull off a chili party is to line up a bunch of slow-cookers. But oddly, my wife didn't think my collection of mismatched, chipped, and permanently stained small appliances looked very elegant. Our disagreement was resolved with the introduction of a new generation of attractive slow-cookers.

The Triple A stainless steel base that holds three individual slow-cooker pots is all you need to feed 8 to 10 folks. Fill one with chili, one with beans, and one with cheese dip or a starch. Arrange the cold condiments on the side.

Linked Pots These stainless steel slow-cookers link up magnetically, only one plug at the end is required, but the heat level for each pot is still individually controlled. If you want to offer chili mac 3-ways, 4-ways, and 5-ways, these are ideal.

Put a couple of different kinds of chili at one end and then add a pot of beans, a pot of chile con queso (page 186), grits, rice, or spaghetti in warm water. Make up a few bowls for early arrivals, so your guests get the idea and then let them serve themselves.

Then put out a basket of tortilla chips, flour tortillas, cornbread (page 185), individual bags of Fritos, shredded cheese, chopped onions, and chopped serranos so your guests can make their own nachos, tacos, or Frito Pies.

Finally, fill a galvanized tub or galvanized buckets with ice and beer and have plenty of tequila and limes on hand.

STONE-GROUND CORNBREAD

Use this moist and creamy cornbread for your "Chili Bubba" (see page 180), or just serve it on the side. It also makes a great tamale pie (see variation below).

MAKES 8 SLICES

2 cups stone-ground yellow cornmeal (such as Anson Mills)

1 teaspoon kosher salt

1 tablespoon sugar

2 teaspoons baking powder

1/2 teaspoon baking soda

1 1/4 cups full-fat buttermilk

2 eggs

1 1/2 cups creamed corn

1 1/2 tablespoons lard or corn oil

Preheat the oven to 425°F. Place a well-seasoned cast-iron skillet into the oven while it preheats. If you don't have a skillet, you can substitute an ovenproof baking dish.

In one bowl, combine the cornmeal, salt, sugar, baking powder, and baking soda and mix well to combine. In another bowl, whisk together the buttermilk, eggs, and creamed corn. Slowly add the dry ingredients to the liquid ingredients, a little at a time, and stir to combine.

With an oven mitt, remove the cast-iron skillet from the oven. Carefully add the lard to the skillet and spread around, then pour in the batter. Bake for about 25 minutes, until the cornbread is golden-brown. Cool for a few minutes, then slice into pie-shaped pieces to serve.

VARIATION

Tamale Pie Grease a 9 by 13-inch baking dish and add 3 cups of the cornbread batter. Spread 3 cups of your favorite chili across the top of the batter in six 1/2-cup dollops. Top with the remaining batter and sprinkle with chopped black olives or jalapeño slices. Bake as directed. Cut into rectangles to serve.

SLOW-COOKER CHILE CON QUESO

Chili con carne's cheesy cousin, chile con queso is also known as "cheese dip" in the Midwest. It's easy to make and serve in a slow-cooker. Ladle over chili, chili dogs, or nachos instead of shredded cheese—or use it as a dip for tortilla chips.

MAKES ABOUT 2 CUPS

1 pound Velveeta cheese, cut into pieces

½ cup shredded sharp cheddar

1 can (10-ounces) original Rotel tomatoes with green chiles

1 cup chicken stock

Combine the cheeses, tomatoes and chiles, and chicken stock in a slow-cooker and heat for 30 minutes on high, or until the cheese melts, then mix well. Turn down the heat to the lowest setting for serving. Stir frequently to prevent scorching.

Keep any leftover dip covered in the refrigerator and reheat as needed.

VARIATION

Salsa con Queso Substitute 1 (16-ounce jar) Pace Picante Sauce for the Rotel tomatoes.

ACKNOWLEDGMENTS

Thanks to Emily Timberlake at Ten Speed Press for keeping things spicy. Thanks to David McCormick at McCormick Literary for service above and beyond, and for the golf lessons. Thanks to Ashley Lima for the fantastic design, and the photo team—Eva Kolenko, George Dolese, Elisabet der Nederlanden, and Glenn Jenkins—for making chili look so good.

Thanks to my daughter and fishing buddy Katie Walsh for her vegetarian recipe development and editing assistance. Thanks to my brother, Dave Walsh for helping me find and critique chili recipes and for taking me deer hunting. Thanks to Jay Francis for the international recipe development and testing and for the fearless chili powder tasting.

Thanks to Dr. Jeff Savell and the gang at Texas A&M Meat Science Center for the free tallow, and all the advice on grinding meat. Thanks to Justin Saunders, Bryan Caswell, and Bill Floyd for the extraordinary efforts to make consistently great chili con carne at El Real Tex-Mex Cafe.

Many thanks to Steven Ryan, grandson of Frank X. Tolbert, for his candor about serving chili with beans at Tolbert's in Grapevine, Texas. And thanks to Mark O. Roberts III and his enchanting wife, Chandra, at Dew Chilli Parlor #2 in Springfield and to Bobby Whitlock at Taylor's Mexican Chili Parlor in Carlinville for the introduction to Illinois chilli.

Thanks to Dann Woellert for autographing my copy of his book, *The Authentic History of Cincinnati Chili*, and for teaching me the right way to eat a three way. And thanks to Todd Varallo of Varallo's in downtown Nashville for the beans with chili. Thanks to the owners of The Texas Chili Parlor in Austin, Ben's Chili Bowl in DC, and the Eat-Rite Diner in Saint Louis for keeping these historic eateries alive.

And thanks to my loving wife, Kelly Klaasmeyer, and our kids, Ava and Joe, for eating so much chili and always asking for more.

Published in the United States by Ten Speed Press,
an imprint of the Crown Publishing Group, a division
of Penguin Random House LLC, New York.
www.crownpublishing.com
www.tenspeed.com

Ten Speed Press and the Ten Speed Press colophon
are registered trademarks of Penguin Random House LLC.
All photos are by Eva Kolenko except as noted on page 193.

Library of Congress Cataloging-in-Publication Data
Walsh, Robb, 1952-
   The chili cookbook : cook-off-worthy recipes for the one-pot classic,
from three-bean to four-alarm, con carne to vegetarian / Robb Walsh ;
photography by Eva Kolenko. — First edition.
     pages cm
   Includes bibliographical references and index.
   1. Cooking (Hot peppers) 2. Cooking (Beans) 3. Chili con carne. 4.
Cooking, American—Southwestern style. I. Title.
   TX803.P46W35 2015
   641.6'565—dc23
                            2015007689

Hardcover ISBN: 978-1-60774-795-6
eBook ISBN: 978-1-60774-796-3

Printed in China

Design by Ashley Lima
Food styling by George Dolese
and Elisabet der Nederlanden
Prop styling by Glenn Jenkins

10 9 8 7 6 5 4 3 2 1

First Edition